FINANCIAL FREEDOM BLUEPRINT

INVEST IN YOURSELF

Side Hustles for as Little as $100

BY SHANNON ATKINSON

CONTENTS

INTRODUCTION

Starting a business can be a difficult and overwhelming endeavor. It requires a substantial amount of time, effort and money. What if there was a way to start a business without investing so much money up front? Here is where the concept of side hustles comes into play.

In addition to your full-time job and other responsibilities, you can engage in a side business or gig. It allows you to generate other income and potentially turn your hobby into a lucrative business. You can kick start a side business with minimal effort and energy without quitting your day job or making major sacrifices.

Where do you even start? It can be hard to determine which of the many potential side gigs best fits you. This is when the book comes into play. We've created a list of side businesses that need minimal time and energy to launch yet have the potential to become profitable services.

Many opportunities are available, from freelancing and consulting to online product sales and service provision. How to market and promote your business and reconcile your side hustle with your full-time work and other duties will be covered.

But there's more. We will also present real-world examples of people who have transformed their side gigs into successful services and suggestions and methods for turning your side gig into a full-time endeavor.

In this BOOK, we will examine the greatest side gigs and services that may be started with minimal effort and time. There is something for everybody on this list, whether you're seeking a way to supplement your income or simply a new and fascinating challenge.

One of the advantages of these side gigs and services is that they may be launched with minimal or no first capital. Many of them can be completed from the comfort of your own home and on a timetable that suits your needs.

Some services on this list may involve a minor investment, such as purchasing materials or equipment. Still, the expenditures are often low compared to conventional brick-and-mortar firms.

If you are ready to kick-start your own business or side hustle, continue reading to learn about 40 viable side hustles or small services that you could potentially start with $100 or $500. These are the greatest possibilities requiring little effort and energy to start.

CHAPTER 1

HOUSE-SITTING OR HOUSESITTING SERVICES

D id you know you can start your own housesitting business? This is a business that anyone, regardless of age or degree, can start. If you truly educate yourself, you can also succeed in this pursuit.

It would likely surprise you to learn how many people seek house-sitting services to assist them with home maintenance while away. Many individuals who depart for extended holidays or work trips don't have somebody to care for their homes. This can provide you with an abundance of business opportunities.

You can simply profit from this opportunity by launching your house-sitting service. You can assemble the individuals who may require this service and provide the individuals who will do the service. Most of the time, you will only need to find people interested in house sitting and houses to sit before you are in business.

However, there is always more to the story, correct? You can earn a profit on a housesitting business if you set your mind to it, even though it will take some effort to pull all of this together and you'll likely need some time.

Listed below are few of the reasons why homeowners seek housesitters:

We live in a dangerous world; an unlocked home is an open invitation for thieves. Therefore, many homeowners engage in a house-sitting service to assist them in identifying trustworthy individuals to guard their homes.

Many people have pets and plants that would die if left unattended for extended periods, requiring the house sitter's attention.

Unattended homes are susceptible to many hazards. Some disasters, such as a leaking roof or a fallen tree, may require the quick attention of a home sitter.

Thus, you now understand why you need to engage home sitters for your business. There are many reasons why someone may want a property keeper and you can benefit from this.

You stand to earn a lot of money if you use your intelligence and launch a house-sitting service. You can start making money quickly while offering excellent service to your clients.

The housesitting industry has been neglected for some time but you can profit from it if you're willing to take a tiny risk and go out on your own.

CHAPTER 2

HANDYMAN OR HOME REPAIR SERVICES

The demand for handyman services is consistently high. There are various services and customers accessible to a handyman, whether a homeowner lacks time to perform repairs himself or a corporate needs regular maintenance of its office buildings (or handywoman) but are there specific things one must know before launching a handyman business?

First, you should ensure that you possess different maintenance, repair and trade abilities. If you already know the fundamentals, taking a class or purchasing a book can help you acquire the knowledge necessary to perform more difficult tasks. This can help you earn more money.

If you are a self-motivated, punctual individual with strong communication skills, you will easily find employment. Handymen who promptly respond to phone calls, are on time and have a pleasant demeanor are more likely to be asked back for other services or suggested to other customers.

It may be easier to raise your income through inventive means. How can you distinguish yourself from other neighborhood handymen while you compete? Perhaps you can provide a quicker response time to phone calls or offer evening or weekend hours.

If you are hired for a position where you can offer consumers money-saving solutions, you can bet that this will grab their attention. Suppose a lack of maintenance necessitates a repair. In that case, you can offer continuous maintenance services for a price so that your client can avoid future repairs, which are typically far more expensive.

Then, how do you start your handyman business?

In addition to being proficient in building, maintenance and repair, the Handyman Association of America can assist you in learning your business. Members of this online community provide advice on home renovation and remodeling projects. Networking with other professionals is an excellent method for obtaining answers to issues swiftly.

1. Interview successful handymen or invest in a basic guide to starting a handyman business that outlines the equipment you'll need, how much to charge customers and how to keep records easily.

2. Gain customers. You want to develop a solid reputation as quickly as possible so you can rely more on referrals and repeat business. So, how do you fast develop a reputation that will attract hiring requests? One option is to register with an online database of handymen, such as Servicemagic.com or Handyman.com.

These database services pre-screen their contractors, allowing customers with repair jobs to browse their websites and locate a trustworthy local handyman. After completing a few jobs and receiving feedback from clients, you have already developed a reputation.

3. Determine the necessary licenses from your local government office. Setting up free consultations with a local insurance agency, banker and accountant (you can acquire references from other local business owners or friends) will provide you with valuable information regarding insurance requirements, financing possibilities and tax-saving tactics.

As a business owner, operating your handyman service can provide many advantages. If you are a problem-solver, enjoy working with your hands and value the independence of working alone, this "job" can be a delightful hobby-turned-career. Thus, there is no better moment than the present to launch your handyman business.

CHAPTER 3

SOCIAL MEDIA MANAGEMENT OR MARKETING SERVICES

You will make money when you identify something people need and want and become the supplier of that product or service. This is true both online and offline. This may sound like basic business knowledge, yet it's how fortunes are earned. Today, I'll demonstrate a problem that has emerged over the past few years and has business owners searching for a solution.

After I unveil it, I guarantee you will have at least heard of it. What you can have forgotten, though, is the immense potential it presents to those who provide a solution. Have you guessed? I'm talking about social media marketing. As a web marketer, I'm sure you've experimented with it.

Most experts concur that it is a beneficial instrument for offline and online business growth. However, the most important features are that it demands talent and ongoing upkeep. Those are the two areas where you can rapidly amass a clientele of individuals willing to pay you to execute the work for them.

Social media marketing is the reason for this aching requirement among business owners worldwide. Everyone is aware that social media marketing is necessary for the health of their business but finding the time to become a social media manager and include it into their already hectic schedules is nearly hard.

"I don't have time for social media marketing" has nearly become a slogan for individuals who are fed up with social media marketing.

What This Indicates

There is a tremendous chance to become a social media manager for firms who can't handle it themselves if your social media abilities are strong or if you are ready to put in the effort to improve them.

With more and more businesses migrating online and requiring a web presence, it is easy to understand how the demand for social media experts is expanding. As more and more platforms come up, the demand for a skilled SM manager will only expand.

Getting Going

The good news is that entering the market as an SM manager doesn't require significant money, time or costly equipment. I chose to share this concept with you after reading about a woman who earns a five-figure monthly income from her cell phone doing this part-time! If she can accomplish this, so can you.

A few excellent low-cost programs will help you learn the abilities you need to provide superior service to your consumers if you require some skill development. Social media management, even part-time, can help your business expand by offering a financial infusion that can be used for other marketing and business needs.

You can quickly become a Social Media Manager with the correct training and guidance, which will assist in funding your MLM marketing and provide you time to let your new business flourish.

CHAPTER 4

E-COMMERCE BUSINESS

With the economy slowly rebounding, e-commerce retailers have become anxious. They are examining and assessing their e-commerce operations and investment initiatives with care. Many retailers, however, are unaffected by this circumstance. Even though the economy is deteriorating, they are adamant that more is still to be gained through e-commerce.

In addition, many e-commerce businesses continue to profit from the expansion of e-commerce sales. Nonetheless, some businesses are implementing plans to strengthen their brick-and-mortar locations to increase their profits. Even though this is the current state of e-commerce, many individuals are nevertheless interested in trying it.

Starting in the realm of e-commerce is difficult. During your first many months in a business, you can suffer frustrations. In addition, if you lack business experience, you can feel overwhelmed by it.

In addition, a lack of Internet-related technological knowledge may hinder the growth of your future firm. Here are some suggestions for launching an e-commerce business to fight these obstacles.

You must secure financing for your e-commerce enterprise. It should not be as high as a typical loan requested by a firm with a brick-and-mortar location. Check with folks that can lend you money without charging excessive interest rates. Alternatively, you can seek out angel investors. They are wealthy individuals who will contribute funding if they believe your business will be successful.

The next step is to locate the cheapest accessible domain registration on the internet. You must use inexpensive web hosting even if you have the necessary funds. Also, when evaluating a web hosting supplier, ensure you comprehend their offerings.

Common web hosting packages include "Basic" and "Business." The 'Business' packages are always ready for e-commerce websites, although the others are not. Choosing the 'Business' option will significantly minimize the work required to create your e-commerce website.

After acquiring a domain for a website, the following step is to construct the website. If you have the necessary skills, you should create them yourself to minimize unnecessary costs. However, if you lack sufficient technological expertise, you should hire freelancers to design your website.

You can open a separate business bank account to keep your personal and corporate finances distinct. Try registering your business as a Limited Liability Business (LLC) to reduce financial risks.

Even if your firm is only starting, you must still hire people. Even if the business is conducted online, some physical labor is required and you can't perform all of it. In addition, you will need the assistance of an accountant for your finances. In addition, you will need a web developer or technician to assist you with your website, particularly when issues arise on your online site.

These are many items. If you adhered to them religiously, your e-commerce hassles would be minimal. Even if the economy is experiencing hard times, you can still succeed in e-commerce.

In conclusion, you must ensure that you have the required number of staff, a cheap Webhosting provider and sufficient funds to launch your future e-commerce business.

CHAPTER 5

PHOTO BOOTH RENTAL BUSINESS

Nowadays, many individuals must consider different means of subsistence. In today's economic context, inventiveness and creativity are occasionally required. If you dream to start a business with low effort and have the necessary funds, it may be worthwhile to investigate photo booth rental.

A skill for sales is required for this type of business. Although this has become increasingly popular recently, many people still find renting photo booths quite unusual and novel. Also, you must realize that variety is the spice of life. Thus, you must provide something that a competitor in the same industry doesn't. Consider that for a moment.

Even though many individuals rent these booths, they nonetheless desire something distinctive and individual. The beautiful thing about these booths is that they can be customized differently. The images it generates are also customizable in that they can be of different designs, sizes and even forms.

Since a photo booth gives fun and a keepsake to people who rent one, this is an important selling feature to remember. Ensure your clients understand that hiring your booth will allow them to have fun and create memories.

The images are also of good quality. They can be uploaded, printed or burned to disc. Most companies that rent out photo booths supply their clients hard copies and digital copies of the images.

This allows clients to submit their memories to a website or social networking site like Facebook. By providing this, you can assure that your clients can access and utilize their images as they see fit. As long as you identify your primary selling factors, your photo booth rental business will be successful. You will require initial funding to acquire the booth.

You will want to choose one roomy, allowing more than one person to fit inside, providing your clients and guests with extra fun, entertainment and photo possibilities. Essentially, you want your booth suited for professional corporate events, parties, and weddings.

In addition, you will need the highest-quality software you can purchase, a digital camera, and the proper printing equipment. These are essential elements without which you can't give quality photographs to your clientele.

Include other products, such as a guest book and some amusing decorations and accessories, if you want to make your photo booth rental business appealing to prospective customers.

If you can afford a wind machine, you should do so without hesitation. The objective is to present your clients with photo opportunities that will result in high-quality, amusing and interesting photographs that they will cherish for a lifetime.

CHAPTER 6

SOAP MAKING

Home-based businesses demand effective marketing and productive production. In the same way bakeries have larger appliances to produce more pastries simultaneously, a soap business needs soap-making equipment to accommodate multiple orders and a continuing financial tracking system to record net profits after accounting for supply costs and expenses.

Don't anticipate online-purchased soap-making kits to allow you to run a soap-making business. Kits for producing your soap for the shower are fantastic for creative projects but they don't contain enough materials and repeated purchases will be costly.

Start with a plan for your handmade soap business:

1. Determine how much you wish to sell and the anticipated profit margin. Set a sufficiently ambitious goal to accommodate future swings in sales and expenses, such as putting money in an emergency savings account.

2. Whether using social media, blogs, advertising or a website, you must identify your target market and sell straight to them.

3. Know the exact cost of operating your soap-making business. Pans, a thermometer, molds and the ingredients for creating handmade soap should be gathered as the initial step in the soap-making process.

4. Calculate the exact cost of each handmade soap product you produce. There are publications available to assist

you in calculating business expenses and developing a sound business strategy for your homemade soap enterprise.

5. When purchasing supplies for handcrafted soap, save money by purchasing in bulk wherever possible. You will need more than a few things at a time and shopping at traditional retail establishments multiple times will be wasteful.

How do you intend to package and sell your stock?

Your neighborhood may or may not be a prime location. Customers who purchase handmade soap want an attractive product that doesn't resemble anything they could get at Walmart. The soap packaging should resemble the upscale soap commonly used in guest restrooms.

If there are other soap manufacturers and boutique stores in your neighborhood, you must remain competitive while still earning a profit. Marketing and packaging are essential to the success of a handmade soap business.

A brick-and-mortar business has higher costs but it may be a successful tool provided the expenditures are well managed and the right advertising techniques are employed. Before assuming you can start a soap-making business from home, conduct research.

Take a course, read some books, and educate yourself on running a homemade soap business. These six steps will help you get started but you'll need to know what you're doing to keep the business afloat and make money on your own.

CHAPTER 7

WHOLESALE SCRAPBOOKING

Have you ever considered joining a scrapbooking direct-sales business merely to receive a discount on your supplies? It might be an effective technique to obtain your product at a discount and mingle with other scrapbookers but it's also essential to review the small print. Here are seven of the most significant considerations:

1. Fashion of products: The most critical consideration is whether or not the product line matches your taste and budget. If you enjoy decorations extensively, certify that the product line includes this. How often are new items introduced?

2. Lessening levels. What is the Instructor/Consultant discount?

Are there any special volume and/or layout requirements for scrapbookers who wish to join the "only for the discount" business? (often referred to as "Hobbyists.")

3. Monthly requirements. What type of monthly personal volume is needed?

If you opt to develop client-specific albums, can you use the discount products in these books? (If the response is affirmative, this is a wonderful approach to expand your profit margin when creating scrapbooks for others.)

4. Initial expenditure. What kind of financial investment will your startup necessitate?

Examine the business's joining fee and/or the expense of your business closely.

Is there any deeper discount on products purchased during the startup phase?

Beginner product packs are often drastically discounted to assist new instructors with their initial inventory requirements. Are these product bundles also available to hobbyists?

5. Does your sponsor accepts hobbyists? Ensure that you will not be pressured if your objective is not to develop a business. Inquire of your prospective sponsor if she invites Hobbyists to join her squad (and make sure that she knows you are one.)

6. Team training. An advantage of joining a group of scrapbooking teachers is the education gained through scrapbooking. Scrapbooking instructors are often imaginative.

Ask your potential sponsor concerning team layout galleries and scrapbooking instruction or chances the business provides.

Are these resources available to both enthusiasts and teachers?

7. Expansion potential. Can this business's hobbyists become instructors?

What are they?

What are the criteria for effecting this change?

Many individuals are astonished by how simple a

Direct sales inevitably develop when they become a source for in-demand, exclusive scrapbooking supplies.

8. Supplies

If you are currently contemplating a direct sales opportunity, please feel free to forward this collection of documents.

Questions to ask your prospective sponsor and good luck finding the suitable firm for you!

CHAPTER 8.

HOME STAGING OR INTERIOR DESIGN SERVICES

There are many considerations to remember if you intend to pursue a profession in house staging. Three major elements must be mastered for the task to be accomplished. Since many house stagers are paid hourly, those keen at pursuing a career in this field must be able to work quickly, accurately and with attention to detail.

Home design should be learned first for a successful profession in interior design. Interior design is the art of changing a property into a sophisticated living area that a buyer may envision themselves inhabiting.

The interior design portion of house staging comprises rearranging furniture, utilizing furnishings already owned by the seller and removing undesired elements such as photographs and travel mementos.

A competent home stager can swiftly examine each room of a home and find the simplest method to utilize the existing components. If adjustments are necessary, such as painting or renting furniture and accessories, the home staging professional can provide good budget-friendly options.

The subsequent component of this profession is landscaping. A skilled stager can assess the curb appeal of a house and offer suggestions for enhancing its allure. Home staging pros will perform small landscaping work and provide advice if the circumstance calls for it.

It is the business of improving the appearance of a house and having it ready to be displayed for sale. It is the same as cleaning and washing your automobile before placing it in front of your house with a "For Sale" sign.

Whether it's a car, furniture or a home, it's quite evident that items that look better sell better. These topics will be discussed in home staging classes. When pursuing certification, you should balance your talents to provide optimal service to your clients.

Certification is the first step in becoming an expert, but you still need to hone your abilities and stage properties to demonstrate your proficiency. The greatest place for a starter stager to start is in their own house, where they can practice combining personal belongings with the requirement to arrange the home optimally.

The expansion of this business has also spurred the proliferation of Home Staging Training courses. Before enrolling in one of these training programs, a person must use discretion, as many appear to be overpriced.

You don't need to invest in inventory or a retail location, making it an extremely low-startup-cost industry. In addition, the sluggish U.S. real estate market may increase the need for home staging services as desperate house sellers seek to avoid the huge price reductions their real estate agents proposed.

You should investigate real estate training if you want certification in house staging. These courses will improve your understanding of the real estate industry, enabling you to become a better home stager.

CHAPTER 9.

FOOD TRUCK OR POP-UP RESTAURANT

A food truck business can be highly lucrative, as many people consume meals from mobile eateries. Instead of waiting for consumers to come to your business, you can go to them and entice them with a unique selection of delicious dishes.

You can kickstart a food truck business with fewer employees than you would need to run a traditional restaurant. Also, it is less expensive and has lower overhead costs than a conventional restaurant operation.

You should start by developing a comprehensive business plan. You must select a precise niche in the food industry regarding the dishes offered and the type of people you desire to attract.

Since most of your business's characteristics will depend on these decisions, you must make them immediately. You must decide if you will sell fast food, soups, ice creams, pastries or different cuisines.

You must also know the age range of your intended audience, be it youngsters, adolescents, college students, CEOs or older folks. Before launching your firm, you must identify your target clients, despite the overlap in age groups.

You must also have a precise business objective in mind.

What will your business look like in five or ten years?

How many other vehicles and personnel would you need?

What kind of income do you anticipate in the future?

These are some of the initial business objectives that you must establish. Once you have a basic idea of what you intend to achieve, you can collect the necessary licenses and permits for your firm.

You must also be aware that certain municipalities prohibit the operation of a food truck business. Therefore, you must choose your business site depending on the local legislation.

After obtaining the necessary permits, you must acquire a food truck for your business. You can buy a used or new truck and rent or lease one for a specified duration. If you need finance for your firm, you can need to locate an acceptable bank or private investor.

Once these are in place, you can immediately start operating your firm. The key to success in the mobile food industry is to be unique and to provide something that no one else does. People constantly want novelty and variation. If you can provide what people require, you can succeed in the food truck business.

CHAPTER 10

HOME BREWING/WINE MAKING

Occasionally, hobbies evolve into something more serious; before you know it, you're running a successful home-brewing business. You have successfully turned your pastime into a business; what else could you want? It would be a dream realized but where do you start?

Millions of people have discovered a fantastic hobby in home brewing. They have already discovered that it is entertaining, simple, cost-effective and profitable.

Where Should You Start with Homebrewing?

Brewing is a hobby that anyone can quickly learn and master. You need some time, some patience and a lot of enjoyment. Most people begin with a home brewing kit, which includes everything necessary for the first batch.

These kits are a terrific method to learn and gain expertise and the resulting beer or wine is exceptional. Most people think of beer when they consider brewing as a pastime but you can also produce root beer and ginger ale.

The following stage is to conduct research.

Before starting home brewing, you must study which ingredients you need, which recipe to employ and the most effective procedures. This is up to personal preference. After researching, you gather the necessary materials and clear your schedule for a few hours. You don't want to become entangled in the brewing process and be forced to quit.

Repeat the process until the flavor is right.

As with any other skill, extensive practice is required before true mastery can be achieved. To refine the brewing process, it is necessary to make mistakes and carefully evaluate each brew. Brewing is not difficult; learning can be much fun when you share your creations with family and friends.

Launch a microbusiness.

Once you have mastered home brewing, you could utilize your newly gained talents to expand your interest. You can launch your microbusiness from the comfort of your home. It would be a good hobby in addition to your profession and you could make money doing it.

The greatest approach to start is to arrange parties for your family and friends, who will be your first and best customers. From there, you can cater parties for the friends of your friends. Your friends who have enjoyed your excellent wine or beer will tell their friends about it, and expand your consumer base through word-of-mouth marketing.

Initial returns on investment would result in modest earnings but this might snowball into a viable firm. Home brewing is an immensely enjoyable pastime but it has the potential to be much more if you give it a try.

If you discover that you truly enjoy brewing or winemaking and have a knack for it, you can always shift into commercial brewing.

Getting Ingredients

Starting to brew your beer is much simpler than you can believe and the results can be remarkable. You will likely wind up with a product that is vastly superior to the diluted beer sold in cans. Purchasing high- quality ingredients are one of the simplest ways to brew a superior beer. Thankfully, the brewing process takes only four materials.

- Hops are the tiny flowers of the Humulus or hop plant.
- Malt extract may be liquid or powdered.
- Specially cultivated grains for brewing beer
- Yeast

You can experiment with different grains, hops and yeast to create your signature beer and a concoction that suits your tastes. The yeast is likely the most essential ingredient in the recipe, as it determines the brewed beer style.

All these ingredients are readily available, but if you are completely unfamiliar with the technique, you can consider purchasing a kit containing all the necessary materials.

Brewing Ingredients

Preparing oneself to make a superb brew requires meticulous planning. Ensure that all components have been measured and prepared in advance. This entails sterilizing all surfaces and kitchen utensils that will come into contact with your brew. Cleaning powders made specifically for cleaning in breweries are worth looking into for sanitization purposes.

In addition to purchasing a notepad and pencil, you can also purchase waterproof writing supplies. This is to keep track of the brewing process so that you can recreate any brew you particularly enjoy and improve the technique for those you don't.

Getting Brewing

The first step is to steep your grains, which you can do in a large grain bag (like a giant tea bag) at 65 degrees Celsius for approximately 30 minutes. Consider that you can also experiment with the duration and temperature at which you soak your grains to perfect your recipe.

The second step is to add the malt extract and start to boil; at this point, the hops are added. Hops are added at varied intervals during the boil to provide distinct flavors.

The final step is to rapidly chill the wort by placing the pot in an ice-filled bathtub and stirring. The wort is then poured into a fermenter and 48 hours later (depending on the recipe), the beer is ready to be bottled.

Unless you have an inexhaustible supply of funds, home brewing can be a very costly pastime, given that the materials range from barely basic to utterly extravagant.

Getting Equipments

This will certainly be the most expensive aspect of your new activity, with equipment ranging from $70.00 to over $400.00; for those of us on a budget, this can be a significant amount of money to come up with all at once.

The local newspaper, online classified ads, pawn shops, garage sales and thrift stores are ideal places to hunt for affordable equipment for home brewing. Sometimes home brewing supplies can be discovered in the most unexpected places. This is because people occasionally want to avoid doing it, so they sell their supplies and equipment at very low prices.

At yard sales, thrift stores, etc., you can typically find airlocks, carboys, buckets, bottles and even labels that can be printed from your computer. Be willing to spend time searching; you haven't selected a quick activity to pursue or start, after all!

An alternative to glass jars and buckets, a 5-gallon plastic bucket will work just as well and is typically free. You can usually obtain 5-gallon buckets for free or at a low cost from your local deli, grocery store or restaurant or buy them brand new at your local home improvement store.

Simply ensure that the buckets have HDPE 2 on the bottom, as this is a common indicator of food-grade plastic, regardless of whether you purchase or receive them for free. In addition, it is essential to avoid using pickle buckets and lard buckets, as the smell of pickles and the grease from lard are impossible to remove.

When purchasing glass for home brewing, it is preferable to purchase new glass. You don't want to wind up with glass jars or bottles that contain chemicals, as there is a high likelihood that they will interact with alcohol or make someone sick. Not a great starting for your new interest!

Yeast can be reused, regardless of whether it is dry or liquid. Save the yeast from the fermenter, store it in glass containers and use a small amount of dry malt extract (any book on the subject will explain how to use it to reuse and preserve yeast). Yeast can be reused multiple times and doing so will save you money if you make your yeast healthier.

As you can see, brewing beer is a rather basic procedure but it takes practice to develop the refined and delicious brews we enjoy. You have nothing to lose by experimenting on a small scale, so get started!

CHAPTER 11

TRAVEL PLANNING AND DESTINATION ADVISORY SERVICES

Travel agents handle all aspects of a trip, including booking flights and hotels, scheduling sightseeing tours, etc.

How to Become a Travel Advisor

After gaining the requisite expertise to handle clients, you can apply for employment in a local travel agency or start your firm. You should preferably possess a high school diploma and it is always advisable to include other academic and professional credentials in your resume.

Since most of the work may be completed online, it is important to acquire transferable skills such as foreign language proficiency and computer literacy. You should have extensive knowledge of travel in general to expand your familiarity with the most prominent tourist destinations, which will be useful for your future career.

Community colleges provide classes that can be advantageous to your career. Enroll in these courses to improve your qualifications. You can apply to firms online or personally by submitting your résumé. Even if they give you a position at the entry-level, you can accept it and work your way up!

What the work consists of:

Assisting vacation-planners in making decisions based on their interests and budget.

By reserving hotels, tickets, cruises and tours in advance, a traveler can avoid dealing with such issues once he arrives at his destination.

He must be able to provide pertinent information regarding the area climate, local customs, passport and visa requirements and currency exchange rates.

In addition to a high school diploma, travel agents must possess destination expertise. They should also be able to conduct Internet searches, as most commerce is now online.

Travel consultants are also expected to participate in familiarization visits to analyze the services and amenities offered in a certain destination before recommending it to their clients.

Consultants are expected to meet with clients and conduct travel-related research via the telephone or the Internet. During summer and spring breaks, they may be required to work longer hours to accommodate the many consumers who hire them to organize their vacations.

The profession of travel agent is highly intriguing. One can pursue a career in the travel industry if one enjoys traveling and discovering new locations. This service is for those who are interested in learning about different locations throughout the globe. This position is ideal for individuals who enjoy communicating with others and traveling.

There are many employment opportunities available and the travel agent is one of them. It is a retail firm that provides services for different travel products on behalf of the primary service providers. These services may include airplanes, hotels, vehicle rentals, cruises, trains and sightseeing tours.

Each year, millions of people travel, making this an expanding sector. There are many advantages to pursuing a career in the travel sector. Listed below are some of the benefits:

The first perk of becoming a travel agent is discovering new tourist destinations worldwide. This is a fantastic profession for someone interested in learning about other parts of the world. As the agent must be current on all information about tourist destinations, this position expands the agent's knowledge.

By utilizing this service, you will have many opportunities to travel. You can use travel groups as a reference to discounts, as travel brokers receive discounts on travel-related products.

Beyond one's wildest imaginings, the travel business is the highest earner. As travel agents receive everything at a discount from the suppliers of the goods and offer the product on their terms, they derive the greatest possible benefits. Therefore, you can amass a fortune by becoming a travel agent.

This job is flexible in that it can be performed anywhere in the world. You can create your travel agency and even work as an online travel agent. This solution is highly adaptable and can be utilized from the office or home.

Possibility to meet new people: this position is ideal for those who enjoy meeting new people and interacting with them. This position offers excellent opportunities to interact with diverse individuals. Therefore, this service is for you if you enjoy traveling and meeting new people.

CHAPTER 12

FURNITURE REFINISHING OR UPCYCLING

Furniture refinishing is the perfect business for you if you possess a garage or other work facility and are interested in learning a craft, re-upholstering or upholstering. This business has two advantages: the initial investment is little and there is always a market for this product or service.

The fact that consumers are discovering new ways to decorate their homes based on the principle of maximizing what they already have is the growth engine for the furniture refinishing industry area.

It is irrelevant if you lack experience in furniture refinishing. Your eagerness to learn about the industry demonstrates that you have a sense of decency. If you are ready to work hard and build outstanding customer relationships, this sense will carry you far in life.

Priority should be placed on furniture refinishing principles for those without experience. It is recommended that starters start with small projects to gain practical expertise in making.

Once confident in their ability to produce quality results, they can gradually take on larger, more challenging projects. You may get paid a small amount initially but if your customers are pleased with your job, you will earn more over time.

To establish a furniture repair business in San Diego, you must adhere to a few fundamental rules to ensure success. Here are some suggestions:

Obtain the Basic Facts:

Simply visit the city's major library to learn about its industries and business trends. Try to obtain study materials on trademarks, service marks and the how-to book category.

Develop a business plan by:

A business strategy is essential for maintaining momentum and achieving goals while competing with colleagues. This plan serves as a blueprint for your future growth and enables you to obtain bank loans for business expansion and other uses. Also, name your business.

Determine the Business's Legal Structure:

Determine whether your firm will be a sole proprietorship, general partnership, partnership with limited liability or Limited partnership. Similarly, it must be registered with the Secretary of State.

Determine the Type of Business Activity:

All registered firms in San Diego must adhere to a specified classification system. This classification establishes the activity type and its prerequisites for initiation. Consequently, while registering your firm, you must specify the activities that will be conducted under the business's name.

CHAPTER 13

CREATION OF PERSONALIZED GIFT BASKETS

A gift basket business is among the most pleasurable endeavors. It can be run from a typical kitchen, requires very little initial investment, and can generate extremely high earnings from local, national and even international customers.

Essentially, you will be responsible for collecting and processing orders from clients seeking unique gifts to give to friends, family and acquaintances for occasions such as birthdays, marriages, housewarmings, christenings, passing your driving test, having a new baby, moving jobs, etc.

Clients come from many walks of life, both private and business and a quality provider that offers innovative, cost-effective designs can attract many return customers.

Until recently, this was a revolutionary service that only a few customers utilized. However, after using a gift basket supplier once, many individuals become addicted to a service that is not only convenient but also extremely individualized.

Jams, candies, cookies, snacks, fruit and other popular delicacies may be included in baskets designed to appeal to many recipients or baskets may be tailored to the specific customer, celebration or event and the recipient's likes and preferences.

WHAT YOU CAN EARN

If you operate locally, nationally or worldwide, whether you produce the contents of the baskets yourself, and what types of baskets and contents you offer will determine your potential earnings.

Profits also rely on whether you offer gifts that appeal to different tastes or whether you select items specifically for each recipient. As for markup, a basket that costs £15 to make should typically be sold for at least £50, if not more.

WHAT WILL YOU BE DOING

You will arrange gifts, confections and foods into baskets. You can purchase containers and contents from outside vendors and make them yourself. Candles, stuffed animals and jams are presented in affordable woven cloth containers, while caviar and silk are nestled in delicately handcrafted baskets.

Most orders will be placed by telephone with credit card payment. You prepare the basket based on the customer's specifications.

How you design your baskets is one of the essential aspects of your business and presentation may enliven even the most mundane goods. Trims and decorations can be bought from the vendors of handicrafts listed below. Alternately, a vast assortment of ready-to-use ribbons, satin flowers, etc. can be purchased.

To put together a modest gift basket

Search for a source of inexpensive, high-quality baskets, preferably unpainted models that you can paint yourself. These should be sprayed or painted with the right hues, such as pink or blue for infants, silver and gold for wedding anniversaries, white for weddings and red and green for holidays. The recipients will want to keep the basket because it is adorned with hand-painted designs. A layer of clear acrylic paint imparts a beautiful gloss.

Consider the proportion between the size and shape of the basket and its contents. Large, shallow, oblong baskets are ideal for food and fruit baskets, etc. The more sophisticated and elaborate the basket should be, the more upscale the contents.

Next, embellish your basket with a decorative lining. For most, tissue paper will be enough, particularly for inexpensive items such as candies, small toys, preserves and jellies. Silk, crushed velvet, patchwork and quilting are acceptable linings for more expensive presents.

Choose the lining based on the gifts and the recipient. Patchwork and quilting are fantastic for infant packs; grass and raffene are ideal for showing Easter eggs; silver and gold paper are useful for many types of sweets, particularly those that are more expensive, etc.

Arrange the gifts in the basket with great regard to aesthetics. Consider how the gift basket will appear in the recipient's house. Flowers, for example, should rise in height toward the back of the basket, as should toys, food, etc.

For smaller things, such as food and canned goods, attempt to arrange the contents so that some are standing, others are lying at an angle, and taller jars and bottles are placed in the back of the display.

Place the basket on a sheet of cellophane large enough to wrap around the container and its contents, leaving a sufficient quantity of cellophane at the top for fastening the gift. Consider whether any last-minute embellishments are essential for the interior of the basket.

Place little crackers in Christmas baskets, faux pearls in wedding and anniversary gift sets, rows of pink or blue beads in baby gift sets, etc. Now, bring the cellophane to the top of the basket, pleat it in an organized manner and secure the top with metallic wire or silver thread. Pull the cellophane until it is taut and all bulges have been gone.

Tie ribbon, ideally wire ribbon, around the basket's rim. With long strings dangling over the cellophane, satin or velvet ribbons look great on pricier baskets, especially when tied to the cellophane.

Again, choose colors according to the occasion and gift: red and green for Christmas, yellow for Easter, white for weddings, blue or pink for newborns, etc. Curling ribbon (either pre-curled or curled over a sharp edge) is a beautiful finishing touch.

Add one prominent piece of décor to the basket, such as a satin rose, a Christmas cracker, a plaque for the nursery, baby shoes, etc.

ADVERTISING YOUR BUSINESS

While a well-established gift basket business will profit from return customers and recommendations, advertising will still be necessary to maintain a consistent flow of new prospects. Advertising will be necessary for those entering the industry for the first time to create a clientele. Here are some promotional strategies for gift basket companies.

Individual Advertising

As a business owner, remember that you are walking advertising for your products. When you meet new people, you might inform them about your line of work and offer them a discount on your items. Always carry your business cards and distribute them at every opportunity.

When you need to give someone a gift, give them one of your creations rather than purchasing something. You will save money and also market your baskets and increase their exposure.

Festivals and Local Events

Look for opportunities to showcase your items in your community. Craft exhibits, fairs and charity events can help you earn sales and establish new relationships with potential clients. People may purchase gift baskets containing non-perishable items on impulse to be prepared for the next time they need a present. Creating a basket that can be auctioned off for charity may also be an excellent way to promote your brand.

Internet Advertising

Many gift basket businesses have marketing strategies that emphasize online advertising. Ensure that your website is fully optimized for search engines and is simple for customers to use and work to generate targeted traffic to it. You will be glad at how much you can accomplish on your own if you educate yourself on online business advertising. Here are some suggestions.

1. Search for online directories that feature local gift basket companies and businesses and submit your information to them.

2. Trade links and banners with local businesses that are not direct competitors.

3. Try pay-per-click advertising using 'Google AdWords' or 'Yahoo Search Marketing' so your ad will appear alongside search results when individuals in your location use specific keywords to search.

4. Have your web developer optimize your website pages for the keywords that customers in your area might use when searching for a gift basket business.

5. Include frequent content on your website that clients will find valuable and attract search engines.

6. Consider creating more web pages on sites such as Hubpages.com, Blogger.com and Squidoo.com. Create content about gift baskets and connect these pages to your main website using your keywords as anchor text. This strategy will assist your website in appearing in search engine results when certain keywords are searched.

Standard business directories

When looking for a business, the 'Yellow Pages' is still one of the first sites people consult. The expenditure may only be justified if the advertisement stands out from the competition. Typically, prospects will only contact one or two organizations before deciding. Therefore, you must have an effective advertisement.

Public Notice Boards

Distribute your flyers across your community. One method is to search for neighborhood bulletin boards that allow flyers or business cards to be attached.

Advertise on your Vehicle

An upfront fee is associated with having a vehicle wrap or magnetic sign manufactured and installed on your vehicle. Once completed, your brand will receive free exposure in your neighborhood for many years.

Local Publications and Magazines

Newspapers often struggle to sell their advertising space so attempt to haggle with them and get a decent offer. If you can get them to write about your firm and benefit from the resulting media coverage, that is even better.

Remember that it may take some time for advertising to start working. Customers may need to read your ad five times before your logo is the first thing that springs to mind when they search for a gift basket provider.

Examine the advertising strategies your more established competitors are employing since they have probably tested them to determine what works and doesn't.

How you advertise your gift basket products will be heavily influenced by advertising. You will boost your chances of succeeding in this field if you give this topic the attention it merits.

SHIPPING AND DELIVERY

Before establishing your gift basket business, you should carefully examine how you ship your products. There are many solutions available and you must research to identify the best possibilities for your business.

In the gift basket sector, it is customary for the consumer to cover delivery costs; another fee is typically added to the bill to cover this. Occasionally, though, transportation costs can be incorporated into the overall gift basket price, allowing an item to be advertised as "free delivery."

There are four primary delivery alternatives: customer pickup, self-delivery, courier, and shipping. Each strategy is explained in detail below.

Customer Pickup

Very few gift basket firms have customers who will pick up their purchased baskets. Some customers may wish to pick up baskets if you have a storefront in a moderately busy area.

Unless you are truly opposed to the hassles associated with clients visiting your business location, you can want to offer them the opportunity to save on delivery fees if they are willing to pick up their items themselves.

Performing one's Deliveries

As a gift basket business proprietor, you can first decide to handle your delivery. This can be an excellent strategy as you observe how customers react to your work and receive feedback. Customers will be able to put a face to your business, which may improve your chances of receiving future orders.

As your business expands, it is unreasonable to believe that you will be able to continue making your deliveries for an extended period because you will be too busy concentrating on other elements of your business.

You can eventually be able to delegate this task to a member of your team. Still, due to the logistics involved, couriers and delivery companies are likely the most cost-effective option (due to the volume of deliveries that will be distributed in an area).

Consider a delivery that may be twenty minutes distant by car and the expenditures connected with labor, gas and other vehicle-related charges. You'll likely realize that it's preferable to outsource your deliveries. For each delivery, local courier rates should range between $10 and $20.

Shipping

For long-distance delivery, UPS or Federal Express should be considered. Compare many options based on their services, which will vary based on delivery time, location, package size and weight (price may also be lower if you drop packages off at your shipper instead of having them pick them up). Prices will vary based on the specifics of each circumstance. Therefore, using the same service for every basket may not be optimal.

If your gift baskets are to be transported, you must preserve them during transport to ensure they arrive undamaged. Obtain a choice of boxes that can readily accommodate your baskets. Wrap each final product with bubble wrap before placing it in a box of the proper size.

Add protective cushioning to the basket, such as crumpled newspaper or foam peanuts. Finally, you can seal the box with tape and label it with a 'This Way Up' sticker to indicate how the product should be handled.

You will probably receive most of your materials in boxed form and you can reuse some of these boxes to save the cost of purchasing so much new packing.

There are many ways to distribute your gift basket designs to your consumers. Consider options that will reduce your problems, ensure that your baskets arrive intact and provide excellent customer service and a fantastic bargain. Delivery is essential to owning a gift basket business, so you should devote time to building a reliable method.

CHAPTER 14

HOME ENERGY AUDITS

Over the past years, "becoming green" has received more attention than in any earlier historical period. There has never been a perfect time than the present to start taking an active role in helping our environment, given the growing body of evidence indicating the detrimental consequences of the greenhouse gases we produce and the genuine concerns of global warming.

Assessing your current carbon footprint is one of the most effective strategies to start assisting the environment. Knowing your current position enables you to start systematically reducing your carbon footprint.

Conducting your own Home or Home-Based Business Energy Audit is a simple and effective approach to identifying areas where you can start to save money. Saving money is a fortunate byproduct of reducing energy consumption. Let's take a moment to examine what an energy audit is and how simple it is to do one on your own.

An energy audit is a survey, an inspection and analysis of energy flow for energy conservation in a structure, process or system to reduce the amount of energy input without compromising output (s). An energy audit is a method for determining how much energy your home or apartment utilizes.

You can easily do a preliminary or basic home energy audit with only a bit of information. With a thorough yet uncomplicated walk-through, anyone may identify many potential problems in virtually any residence style.

Remember, maintain a checklist of locations investigated and issues discovered when auditing your house. This list can assist you in prioritizing your energy efficiency improvements.

Air leaks and drafts are one of the most prevalent causes of energy loss in the home. Potential energy savings from eliminating drafts in a home can vary between 5 and 30 percent per year and the home is typically much more pleasant afterward.

Start with doors and windows. Check for interior leaks, such as gaps along the baseboard or floor's edge and the seams between walls and ceilings. Always pay attention to electrical outlets, switch plates, fireplace dampers, attic hatches and window frames and the weather stripping around external doors.

Inadequate insulation or, in some cases, no insulation is a significant contributor to heat loss in your residence. If the insulation levels in your home don't meet the minimum requirements, heat loss through the ceiling and walls might be substantial.

If your home is older than 10 years, you should comprehensively assess the attic insulation. Ensure that the attic is adequately ventilated, as optimal air circulation is vital to the overall performance of your home's heating, cooling and ventilation system (HVAC).

Wall insulation inspection can sometimes be more difficult than attic insulation inspection. There are methods for evaluating wall insulation, such as locating inconspicuous areas to cut a hole in the sheetrock and inspecting what's within the wall.

This method is not always accurate. Hiring a professional energy auditing firm to do a Thermographic Wall Inspection is likely the most thorough method for inspecting wall insulation. The heat loss within the wall or other building envelopes is measured using an infrared scanning instrument.

Next, inspect your home's heating and cooling equipment annually or as the manufacturer advises. Regularly inspect and replace furnace and A/C filters. When evaluating your HVAC system, you should pay particular attention to the ductwork and all air returns and chases. Again, if your home is older than 15, you should consider upgrading to a more energy-efficient HVAC system.

Lastly, lighting contributes roughly 10% of your monthly electric expenditure. Be sure to inspect the wattage of the light bulbs in your home. Consider where you can cut the power of your light bulbs and replace them as they burn out with the new compact-fluorescent lamps (CFL), especially in locations where lights are left on for hours.

Don't forget to contact your local electric utility business. An increasing number of utility companies offer rebates and incentives for purchasing and using energy-efficient appliances, lighting and devices.

Consult the local yellow pages for a thorough and expert Home or Home-Based Business Energy Audit. You can also save money by maintaining a commitment to reducing your carbon impact.

Energy auditing is a viable alternative for anyone interested in a stable and environmentally friendly job.

Even during economic downturns, when individuals are more focused on saving money, this industry is anticipated to continue to develop. This virtually guarantees your job stability, regardless of the broader economic picture. Energy auditors enjoy many substantial benefits. You can be your employer and training can be simple and quick.

What are the startup costs? Minimal.

Also, you can position yourself at the forefront of an emerging energy-saving trend. Your energy auditing business might be a local leader in this burgeoning industry.

Different novel business concepts

Training as an energy auditor opens the door to different professional prospects. Some examples include:

Independent Home Energy Auditor

- Gives domestic energy efficiency recommendations
- Independent Business Energy Auditor
- Gives energy efficiency recommendations for commercial buildings
- Auditor of energy efficiency engaged by a utility business

You would deliver monthly energy audit recommendations to utility business consumers. Now that utility companies see the demand for energy audits, they provide it as an other service to their customers. This accurately reflects the expansion of the energy auditing business.

An alternative energy-specialized energy auditor

People interested in installing an alternative energy system (such as solar, wind or geothermal power) on their land might seek your energy guidance. Consumers often want assistance in comprehending how to optimize these systems and successfully integrate them with other energy sources.

An energy auditor who specializes in the design and construction of buildings

You would advise builders and architects on how to increase the energy efficiency of buildings. They may also undertake assessments of freshly constructed properties to give investors an energy rating. This is an essential component of the energy audit business, as investors are increasingly interested in a property's energy efficiency before purchasing it.

Because conducting energy audits is such a young profession, you have a lot of leeway in determining your career path.

Examine the components of many training programs to select the one that best corresponds to your interests.

When investigating the finest energy audit training programs, check whether they provide modules on the general concepts of running a firm. You will need marketing, taxes and public relations knowledge to successfully run an energy audit business.

Consider whether a respected organization has authorized the course. For instance, certification from the National Energy and Sustainability Institute (NEASI). This indicates that you can take the NEASI Home Energy Audit Certification Exam after completing the course. This certification improves the legitimacy of your business.

CHAPTER 15

ONLINE ACCOUNTING OR BOOKKEEPING SERVICES

Suppose you have a flair for dealing with numbers and experience as a part-time or full-time bookkeeper. You can give yourself an automatic raise by learning to establish a profitable accounting business from home.

Thousands of local and online small companies immediately demand your services. While many business owners use accounting software to handle their records, most prefer outsourcing this. Finding these business owners and acquiring them as clients is among the most important aspects of freelance bookkeeping success.

Now, I'm going to assume that you have years of bookkeeping experience. To be competitive in this field and present oneself as a true professional, you must have at least two to five years of business bookkeeping experience.

There is no way to fake your degree of experience since business owners will inquire about it immediately. Before promoting this service, you'll require on-the-job training if your bookkeeping skills are only basic.

We live in a more entrepreneurial age where it is easier than ever to establish a business and an increasing number of people are seizing this chance. Consequently, there are also increasing opportunities for those who give services to businesses.

Whether you are a chartered accountant and business consultant or have no qualifications but have expertise maintaining books for a firm and access to software, you can establish your own business and start earning money but how should it be accomplished?

First, if you're aiming for a low-cost start-up, you'll likely be operating online and advertising your business in this manner, as it's much more cost-effective. You must discover a niche to succeed in this endeavor and distinguish yourself from the competitors you will confront in the online marketplace.

It may be a false niche, mainly for marketing purposes and offering the same services as any other but it will still be helpful. An individual may search online for bookkeeping services for a specific business; here is your opportunity to stand out.

Also, suppose you can do some good research. In that case, you can establish yourself as a bit of an expert in the field, offering business advice to people in that one specific area and if you can get known this way - by giving something away for free (knowledge), that can be a great way to not only get yourself noticed but to have people associate your name or the name of your business with good advice and professionalism, making them want to hire you and use your services even more.

To be able to do this, you will need a website. Still, you can get one for next to nothing and writing and publishing articles like this costs nothing as well - so it is possible for a person to get started in this industry, start receiving work and generate an income without spending a dime. No investment implies no risk; therefore, you have nothing to lose.

Okay, so you already possess the necessary skills and want the flexibility to work from home on your own time, right?

Developing a viable business plan is the initial step. This need not be elaborate; you can simply create a list of things to perform to establish your firm. In addition, you must men-

tion strategies for selling your services to potential customers.

Due to the availability of advanced accounting software,
you can cater to local clients or expand your service to internet clients. To be online, you will also need to learn how
to operate a bookkeeping firm online. This primarily entails
creating a website that offers your services. Also, there are
some web locations where you can bid on private bookkeeping jobs.

Among the benefits of freelancing is that if you reach a
particular level of experience, you can earn more money.
The greater your professional expertise, the higher you can
charge clients. Wouldn't you want to earn $30 per hour do-
ing what you're doing now?

CHAPTER 16.

VIRTUAL OR PHYSICAL COOKING CLASSES

Cooking classes are currently gaining popularity. There has been a soar in the number of persons seeking cooking instruction. If you are a competent chef with a strong desire to share your culinary talents with others, founding a cooking school is an excellent career option to consider.

A culinary lesson is a win-win proposition. You inspire your culinary novices to learn this art and earn a respectable salary from this endeavor. Here are other tips for running a successful cooking class:

1. Academics

Knowledge is an unbeatable asset when launching a new business. Many factors must be considered when organizing a cooking class. Diverse reading resources on cooking classes and food enterprises can provide you with the necessary direction.

2. Business Plan

You can move on to the following step, which is creating a business strategy if you have acquired sufficient knowledge through research. In planning, emphasis is placed on multiple factors. This covers the materials you must prepare, the initial budget you must allot, the anticipated income and the location of your classes. Rent for businesses with expansive kitchens.

Also, you must determine the class size. Also, you must consider how much you will charge your students. You must also determine how long the culinary course will last per day and how often it will be held per week.

3. The use of constructive criticism

Consult those who are knowledgeable and experienced in the subject of culinary instruction. Try presenting them with your business plans. You can also solicit feedback and suggestions from your family and close friends.

4. Food Security Certification

Now that you have a plan, you can obtain a certification in food safety. This certification is necessary for all food businesses. It demonstrates your culinary credibility. The state could fine you severely if you did not receive food safety training before teaching a cooking lesson.

5. Marketing

Similar to television advertisements, you must also publicize your intention to teach a culinary class. You can distribute flyers, booklets and business cards to recruit new members.

You can post flyers in important locations such as schools, restaurants and supermarkets. It is a marketing strategy to provide introductory discounts and freebies to attract more pupils.

6. Recipe

After all the intricacies, you must select a recipe with which you are quite familiar. Ensure that you are comfortable teaching and preparing this recipe in front of your pupils. An experiment in your kitchen.

Every step should be recorded on a pad of paper. These instructions will be typed beside the ingredient list. Both will be included in the printed recipe that will be distributed to your pupils after the class.

7. Plan in Advance

You should avoid wasting time. Gather the necessary ingredients and equipment before class starts. Ensure that the kitchen cookware is carried to the cooking class location. Prepare sufficient food samples in advance. The samples provide the pupils with a sense of the desired flavor.

8. Orientation

The day of the real culinary class arrives. Introduce yourself, your kitchen policies and the goals you intend to achieve by the end of the culinary course as the class starts. Demonstrate the recipes with grace, enthusiasm and flair. Be receptive to your pupils' inquiries and explanation requests.

9. Commencement

As the cooking class concludes, present the printed recipe you prepared in advance to your pupils. This will give your students a recipe to practice and adapt at home. In addition, a photo of the finished dish can be sent.

The passion of one man is infectious. You can share your enthusiasm for food with a large audience through culinary workshops. Despite the difficulties, the satisfaction of encouraging a novice to cook fully is priceless. Indeed, a bit of research, a modest demonstration of your culinary prowess and a passion for teaching are the fundamental first stages in starting a cooking class.

So, what are the prerequisites for a cooking class?

First and foremost, you must exhibit exceptional cooking talents. Unless your credentials impress potential students, your class will likely have no participants.

You can publicize your abilities and accomplishments by distributing pamphlets or hanging a banner in front of your business. In addition, don't forget to include your contact information so interested registrants can make queries.

Before announcing your culinary course formally, you must also organize your courses in advance. Whether focusing on pastries and baked goods, gourmet foods or Italian cuisine, the style of cooking you aim to teach must be distinct enough to attract market attention.

People will likely inquire about the course outline before enrolling and if you don't present them with a thorough synopsis, they will lose interest in enrolling.

Next, invest in essential cooking supplies. Spatulas, spoons, chopping boards, knives and other typical kitchen equipment must be given to improve your pupils' learning experience.

Also, you should ensure that the amount of space at your venue is proportional to the number of attendees you want to welcome. Such amenities as sinks, ovens and stoves should be present and functional. Remember that the registration fee should cover the costs of procuring these items.

Pre-registration is also advantageous. Pre-registration is an easy approach to anticipating the size of your class and also helps offset the initial expenses you have incurred. It can even improve the flow of your class on the first day since you can offer the students pre-printed name tags.

Thus, the designated time for the first day will be spent on the formal orientation and not on pre-registration or waiting for other students to arrive.

You can also invite more people by offering perks such as discounts or gift certificates to the first few registrants or by providing free extra hours of special cooking instruction to those who can pay the full cost upfront.

CHAPTER 17

YOGA/MEDITATION INSTRUCTOR

So, you wish to establish a yoga school. People from many walks of life have a substantial incentive to become yoga teachers, teach as independent contractors, open yoga schools or quit their day occupations due to the widespread appeal of yoga.

However, what appears simple to many requires planning. Businesses open and close within a few months for different reasons, including poor locations, lack of a business strategy, insufficient startup capital and inadequate marketing expenditures.

Obtaining Credentials

According to industry standards, the first step in starting your yoga school is to receive certification as an instructor from a recognized university. Certification typically necessitates an intensive education. Nobody was certified for years until yoga instructors realized they could be sued.

In certain countries, litigation is comparable to a lottery. Today is a lucky day because you can sue anybody for anything. Some individuals meticulously prepare and scheme for the opportunity to take anyone to court, while lawyers adore it.

What can yoga instructors do? Acquire certification, liability insurance coverage and a track record of safe methods in your classes. Registration is a possibility. However, it is typically not necessary for liability insurance.

Sincerely, some teachers (who are neither trained nor registered) own sports liability insurance. However, certification demonstrates that you have rigorous training in teaching yoga sessions safely. Therefore, this improves your trust as a yoga instructor who prioritizes student safety.

Create an action plan

Once you are certified, investigate the rates for yoga instruction in your demography to remain competitive and build a business plan! In addition, you must determine if you wish to be the sole proprietor, a partner, or incorporate or operate a limited liability business for your yoga school.

It is essential to determine the specifics of this aspect of the business, as the annual income of new instructors can range from $30,000 to $70,000. As a lone proprietor, you can cultivate a private clientele to acquire exposure and establish rapport, which may prove more profitable.

There is also the possibility of working as a freelancer. As an independent contractor, you can work as a sole proprietor from an existing location, such as a private health club or fitness center, with an established customer to save the overhead costs of renting your building and hiring staff.

You must also decide which type of yoga you will specialize in and teach at your school. People in a fitness club may not engage in yogic breathing or meditation, preferring yoga's physical flexibility and strength training aspects. Vinyasa, Hot Yoga, Ashtanga and Power Yoga are well-liked yoga exercises for fitness centers.

Regardless of the course a yoga business chooses, the following considerations are essential: Obtain the certificates and permits required to get started, decide on a marketing strategy and the sort of yoga that would best fit your consumers, then advertise your business accordingly. Also, get insurance that covers the type of yoga school you operate to safeguard your legal position.

According to ancient yogic philosophy, doing a business a reality takes a lot of commitment and effort. Beyond the poses, meditation, spiritual enlightenment, mantras and breathing techniques, yoga is becoming an enterprise, according to the New York Times. The everyday management of time, energy, people and money is the source of the drama. If you believe being a yoga instructor has nothing to do with

Many individuals have adopted yoga as a type of exercise and developed a fondness for it due to its increasing popularity. Most people have also begun to view it as an excellent vocation. Yes, becoming a yoga instructor would be a profitable profession for you.

It will improve your passion, keep you in good health and offer you a substantial amount of money.

If you are serious about becoming a yoga instructor, here are some critical and straightforward measures you can take to achieve your goal:

- Procedures for becoming a yoga instructor

1) Step one

The first and most essential method is regular meditation. In this manner, you would explore many styles of yoga. The entire procedure will help you acquire the most valuable experience possible.

2) Step two

To excel as a yoga instructor. The study of yoga's history and philosophy is essential. This will improve your understanding of this exquisite art considerably. This is the most effective technique to impart a deep grasp of yoga to your students.

3) Step three

To realize your aspiration of becoming a yoga instructor, you must attend every workshop. This will advance both your education and practice. These brief sessions are essential for sharpening your abilities.

This facilitates networking with your friends. Some seminars are designed to provide great teacher training and practical classroom management experience.

4) Step four

Finding a qualified yoga instructor is the greatest method to hone your skills and transform yourself.

Attend a program designed specifically for educating yoga instructors. You can effortlessly network with top-tier yoga teachers who are currently operating studios as your skills improve. You would learn how to run a successful firm in this manner.

5) Step five

You must continue working with your mentor until he determines you are prepared to move on.

6) Step six

Learn helpful tips for organizing your yoga practice planning. You can be an expert in your techniques, but you still need to learn things from a seasoned professional in your sector.

7) Step seven

After becoming a yoga instructor, you must pick where you will teach. Some people like to create their tiny studios, while others prefer to train at home.

8) Step eight

In the United States, to become a registered or certified yoga instructor, you must pass two levels of yoga alliance certification. The duration of these stages is 200 and 500 hours, respectively.

Follow the steps outlined above and you'll be well on your way to becoming an accomplished yoga instructor.

CHAPTER 18

PRODUCT SOURCING/ DROPSHIPPING

One of the best chances for launching a business quickly is to start a dropshipping business. This business may be handled from the comfort of your home, as you will never have to stock inventory or transport things.

You only need to create a website or post your drop-ship products on eBay to start selling. Once they sell, you transmit the order to the drop-ship provider, who then ships the product to your buyer, allowing you to retain a substantial profit.

There are currently a large number of people adopting this dropship business strategy online. Some earn six-figure salaries, while others work part-time in addition to other employment. People then discover that their dropship business is so successful that they can quit their day jobs.

There are no unique abilities required to establish a dropshipping business. A willingness to succeed requires a computer and an internet connection. Then, you establish contacts with a dropship supplier and commence online sales via your website or eBay auctions.

Why are the Phases of Starting a Dropshipping Business Important?

Dropshippers confront some of the same obstacles as other business owners and dropshipping is a business that requires research, preparation and experience. Before you start dropshipping things, you must thoroughly understand what you'll be doing. Finding a hungry market is the initial step in launching a dropshipping enterprise.

How to Dropship Products: Initial Steps

There is no use in attempting to drop ship unwanted things. Don't commit to selling a specific product until you have conducted adequate keyword and product-sourcing research.

Examining your competitors is one technique to determine whether your product is in demand. Enter your product's keywords into a search engine such as Google. If many advertisements are on the right side of the results page, there is likely a demand for your goods.

You will also need to visit a dropshipping directory to locate reliable dropshippers who stock and ship the products you're attempting to sell. When starting a dropshipping business, watch out for scammers.

The benefit of dropshipping is that you don't need to maintain any inventory; you simply need to wait for a customer to place an order and receive payment before the goods are dispatched.

How to Dropship: Intermediate Steps

You can sell your things online by establishing a website that functions as your storefront. As soon as you start selling, you'll discover what sells and what doesn't. Offer more of the things that sell well and avoid selling those that don't. You can suffer delays if your dropshippers don't have items in stock. You must inform your customers of these delays as soon as possible.

On your website, you must implement a pre-built shopping cart solution, such as Zencart or Yahoo M. Both options enable you to create an eCommerce website with no programming skills. Yahoo Merchant Solutions will manage your payment processing starting at $39.95 per month. Zencart is free to use but payment processing must be set up independently.

How to Dropship Items

Order fulfillment is one final step in launching a dropshipping business. The benefit of letting the supplier handle order fulfillment is that you will not incur the added expense of holding the merchandise. You will also be provided with bulk shipping rates, which may differ from ordinary costs by as much as 30 percent.

After determining order fulfillment with your drop shipper, you must focus on price. You will purchase the products at wholesale costs and must determine your desired markup percentage. Be wary of dropshippers that charge fees, as this will increase the price of your products for clients.

Remember that legitimate wholesale drop shippers may ONLY be discovered in a drop ship directory. A Google search for drop shippers will return some con artists and middlemen whose sole goal is to separate you from your hard-earned cash.

Dropshipping enterprises are gaining in popularity and many people are generating substantial salaries from the comfort of their own homes. This type of enterprise necessitates extensive research, efficient advertising and customer satisfaction.

Due to the internet-based nature of dropshipping businesses, thorough research is required to avoid scams. Check references that attest to the business's dependability and ensure that it has adequate security measures to protect credit card users.

When you have reduced your search to two or three wholesalers, acquire a selection of each product to familiarize yourself with their offerings. It is essential to conduct demographic research to determine which products are and is not available in your area. Identify a niche for the things you intend to market before placing an order. Certainly, research is required for this type of firm.

To ensure the success of your business, you must promote the things you sell. Enrolling in a course on public speaking will enable you to converse with consumers easily. Hosting a party to showcase products is an effective method of advertising. Whether your event is a ladies' afternoon tea or a men's backyard BBQ, the ambiance will be conducive to promoting your business.

Possessing an exhibit at farmer's markets, mall kiosks or flea markets is also a fantastic advertising approach, as shoppers in these locations often seek out the unusual. Leave your business card with as many people as possible. Advertising exposes your firm to potential clients.

Most essential, ensure the satisfaction of your customers. After each sale, take the time to follow up with your consumers. This will significantly improve the number of repeat consumers since they will feel more comfortable purchasing from someone who values their feedback.

This phone conversation or email will also allow you to hear their candid opinions regarding the things you sell. If the business whose product you sell repeatedly provides the incorrect order, the goods are of low quality or delivery is often late, it is time to look elsewhere.

Starting a dropshipping business may be both profitable and exciting. Your firm will be successful if you conduct thorough research, use effective promotional methods and ensure client happiness.

CHAPTER 19

RENT A ROOM THROUGH AIRBNB

A bed and breakfast is a modest motel that offers overnight accommodations and typically includes breakfast at the rate. Based on the European tradition of hospitality, classic B&Bs are often family homes, although the concept has been stretched to encompass self-contained accommodations and cottage rentals.

The accommodations might range from a room in a private residence with shared amenities to a multi-bedroom luxury vacation cottage.

B&B startup costs:

When developing a business strategy for a bed and breakfast, it is essential to include renovation expenses. Many of these expenses are tax-deductible, as are recurring costs such as power, property taxes and maintenance.

A wise business owner will not overcapitalize, instead utilizing existing features and renovating when cash flow is strong. Determine your return on investment (ROI) and the years it will take to generate a profit. It may be important to augment your B&B income in the short term.

Attributes of a quality bed and breakfast inn:

A bed & breakfast inn should be well-appointed, immaculate and equipped with contemporary facilities. A placement adjacent to local attractions and natural places of beauty will improve the number of inquiries you receive.

Good B&Bs should feature off-street parking, air-conditioned rooms with en suite bathrooms and TV/DVD/CD players in each room. A guest lounge where guests can relax, converse and play games is unquestionably an asset. B&Bs should have wireless internet access (wifi) to match modern travelers' expectations.

Delivering superior customer service:

A successful bed and breakfast will provide a hospitable environment where guests feel at ease and well cared for. Essential qualities include the capacity to handle emergencies, adaptability and effective communication abilities. Always react quickly to email inquiries and greet callers with a smile.

The breakfast menu should be diverse, featuring alternatives for gluten-free and wheat-free diets, among other dietary restrictions. Towels and sheets must be immaculate and rooms must be serviced regularly.

Always look for ways to exceed your customer's expectations by providing other services such as fresh flowers in the guest rooms, restaurant reservations, cab service and extra meals upon request.

Your guests will be more likely to suggest you to their friends if you have a solid grasp of the surrounding area and can provide them with brochures and advice on tourist activities.

How to market your inn:

Send regular advertisements for your bed and breakfast to your local tourist organization. Attending local functions and community activities will increase your credibility among local businesses and community groups.

It is crucial to have an online presence with a well-designed website linked to local tourism directories. Prepare media kits with information about your bed and breakfast, including reservation information, rates, photographs of guest rooms and information about area attractions.

CHAPTER 20

CREATE AND SELL UNIQUE T-SHIRTS ONLINE

There are different ways to sell custom-designed T-shirts online. The shirts should feature a statement or graphic that people will want to wear because they associate it with something positive or something they want to promote themselves.

Custom T-shirts don't require a substantial financial investment. You can locate a website that not only allows you to purchase these shirts for significantly less money than you might expect but also allows you to design your unique T-shirts.

Utilizing an interactive website makes the process of designing personalized T-shirts much simpler. You can view the shirt's appearance before placing an order and selling the shirt online. There are many ways to accomplish this. Here are many examples:

Sell them on online auction sites

If you have a message or graphic on your custom T-shirts that you believe many people will want to wear for themselves, you can sell the shirts on websites that allow you to sell things to individuals worldwide. Even if you've never sold a product, selling anything on auction websites is simple. Websites are extremely user-friendly and make it simple to sell bespoke T-shirts.

Sell them on your social media profile.

If you have a page on a social networking site dedicated to a cause or similar to a fan club, you can sell custom T-shirts on this site to raise money for your cause or club. On your social networking site, you can sell t-shirts that reflect the opinions of others towards your friends. You can even use this to raise funds for a good cause.

Sell them on the Internet.

You can easily incorporate personalized T-shirts if you have a website dedicated to a cause, a celebrity, or even sales. One of the advantages of selling personalized T-shirts on your website is that you can accept orders, place the order with the manufacturer and just pocket the profit.

There are many online moneymaking opportunities. Selling personalized T-shirts online is just one way to utilize the internet to your advantage.

CHAPTER 21

SELL HOMEMADE BEAUTY ITEMS MADE FROM NATURAL INGREDIENTS

Follow these step-by-step instructions to create your brand of cosmetics and skincare products. Find your niche and make luxury, pampering items without leaving your home!

Product Improvement

What's your specialty?

What do you love?

What specific demands does your skin have?

What would enthrall your loved ones?

What will distinguish your products from those of your competitors?

You can already know the answers to these questions but if you don't, use the internet to help you establish your vision for your skincare!

The choices are limitless; will you establish a line of products for mothers and infants, males and adolescents?

Will you utilize indigenous Australian products, botanicals and essential oils?

Will you concentrate on natural or organic skin care products or the therapies they provide?

Will you expand into an exclusive market or offer more affordable products?

If you are ready to start building your skincare, you already have a passion for some aspect of the industry; therefore, you should utilize your strengths to create a unique niche.

Choosing Your Ingredients

Consider your niche when selecting products; this will help to reduce costs and prevent impulse purchases. If you are designing a product for aged skin, butter and cream bases will better fit your needs than lotions. Check the safety precautions of the products you're contemplating if you're designing skin care for moms and infants to verify they're appropriate for newborns or pregnancies.

Sites providing bulk base products, raw materials and other skin care necessities in Australia will describe the quality of each item, the types of products the raw component is used in and the percentage to be added to your base product. If you can't discover the information you require, you can either send them an email with a question or conduct your Internet research.

Simple Internet searches can yield many listings of essential oils, hydrosols, exfoliants, extracts, raw ingredients, and preservatives and a description of the product's properties and purposes.

Initially, it would likely be simpler and cheaper to purchase pre-made body butter, lotions, gels and scrubs from suppliers and add your raw ingredients to create your specialized range. As a general rule, when adding more raw materials to your base product, regardless of whether you prepared it yourself or bought it ready-made, a concentration guideline is -

Essential oils total - Eye area - 0.25% (5 drops per 100ml), Face - 0.25 - 1% (5 to 20 drops per 100ml) (5 to 20 drops per 100ml), Body - 1-2% (20 to 40 drops per 100ml) (20 to 40 drops per 100ml), Feet - 2% (40 drops per 100ml) (40 drops per 100ml)

Other total oils (including rosehip, evening primrose, etc.) -1% to 10%

Total extracts (calendula, cucumber, etc., extracted into glycerin) -0.6% per 100 ml (1-6 ml)

1% to 10% total hydrosol (floral waters)

Exfoliants total (jojoba beads, walnut shell, etc.) 1% to 5% of finely ground exfoliant for the face, 5% to 10% of medium to coarsely ground exfoliation for the body

This is largely dependent on the intended use of your product. Small amounts (up to 2%) can be used in cleansers or creams to detoxify skin or to add color to your product. Larger levels can cause the product to thicken after application and are therefore better suited for facial masks and body wraps that will be removed after drying.

The number of available additives is practically unlimited; therefore, you should investigate those chemicals that you believe will provide the greatest value to your users while remaining within your budget.

If you are having problems selecting additives, research other skincare or beauty products developed in the area you're interested in to see what they've decided to use and how they've mixed essential oils, clays, extracts, powders, etc. to make specialized products.

While research is essential, ensure that you don't replicate another recipe or build a clone of a product for sale - all websites and shops have copyright over their products, so utilize your research to develop your ideas and acquire your devoted customers!

Enjoy producing your goods and learning how to launch your own natural skincare business.

By starting a home-based business selling natural health care products from the comfort and convenience of your own home, you can not only eliminate the stress and hassle of commuting, punching time clocks and dealing with employers' power trips but you can also finally start earning the type of income you deserve while providing a valuable product to those who need it.

You can start selling beauty items immediately with nothing more than a telephone and a pad of paper. The natural health care products market has never been better than it is now due to heightened knowledge of the presence of toxic chemicals in many commonplace products.

CHAPTER 22

LAWN CARE OR GARDENING SERVICES

When most entrepreneurs consider launching a lawn care business, one of the first things that come to mind is whether or not they can earn a "six-figure" income with a lawn mowing service.

It is feasible to generate a pre-tax salary of more than $100,000 from a lawn care service's revenues; some can earn much more. However, even more lawn care service owners never quite "get it" and struggle to earn a living salary despite their efforts.

Basic Start-Up Equipment

If you are a conscientious enthusiast who views gardening as a hobby rather than a chore, you can turn this passion into a lucrative lawn care business. The first, perhaps costly step in establishing this lawn care business is acquiring expensive equipment.

However, you are not required to purchase the equipment immediately. Acquiring the fundamental tools first is recommended for a start-up lawn care business, provided that they are efficient enough to manage your operations. This is because you still need to develop your client base.

Also, it is not prudent to incur debt to purchase lawn care business equipment that has not yet been utilized. Consequently, you should first focus on acquiring the fundamental equipment for a lawn care business: a lawn mower and an edger.

The Lawn Cutter

This is considered the lifeblood of a lawn care company, so quality must be the deciding factor when choosing one. However, for a new firm, you must also adhere to your operational budget. Commercial-grade lawnmowers are priced at $2,000 or more.

There are further possibilities for folks with limited funds. One option is to use a regular lawn mower, typically used in residential areas. With this equipment, you can target clients with similar lawn equipment, such as newly constructed homes, condominiums and small apartments.

Maintaining your lawnmower is essential, as it is the lifeblood of your lawn care business. This can be accomplished by regularly sharpening the blades and repairing the machine.

Your lawn care firm must have a mulching bag. It is a protective coating that prevents grass remnants from being carried away. Investing in more advanced lawn care equipment is now possible using the funds gained from completing first minor jobs.

The Edger

Another basic item to start your lawn care business with is the edger. It offers that sheen to your lawn after a mowing session. An edger fueled by gasoline is recommended for your lawn care business. In addition to not requiring electricity from the client, it is conveniently transportable and capable of performing well.

There must be elements that differentiate successful 'six figure' operators from the rest. In the following essay we have sought to discover those aspects that make certain lawn businesses excellent while others never amount to much.

1. Strive to have exceptional knowledge of lawn maintenance, lawn mowing and the equipment used if you want to appear professional when you meet prospects. To manage an operation that maximizes efficiency, you must thoroughly grasp the business's practical aspects.

2. Successful lawn care professionals prioritize brand marketing. This is all about establishing your market reputation. Your brand will gain value if you continue to deliver on its promise, allowing you to acquire clients more readily. Name and logo are significant but how your market perceives you and the type of company you come to be perceived as will be much more essential.

3. Organize your time effectively and use processes to save time and run your business more efficiently. A good information processing software system for your lawn care business will allow you to stay on top of your paperwork and provide data that will improve your understanding of your business. Your firm's performance in the past can inform future decisions of significance.

4. Sales and marketing are essential to any sector, including the lawn care industry. Package your services in a way that shows the customer the value you offer and learn how to price your services in such a way that maximizes revenue. Test a range of advertising strategies to find cost-efficient ones and create a sales approach that increases the number of leads you can turn into new accounts.

5. It is usually easier to sell to your existing customer base than to gain new customers. Learn how to market extra, premium, and more frequent services to your clientele. Find home, garden and property-related services with strong profit margins in demand in your area and promote them in addition to basic lawn mowing.

6. Acquire as much knowledge as can about lawn care, the lawn care industry and basic business marketing and management. Read books and e-books written by suc-

cessful lawn care providers and look for a mentor willing to coach you for an affordable charge.

7. Recognize that once you have established yourself, your clients will refer you to their friends. To reap the benefits of word-of-mouth marketing, you must serve your customers effectively and give them many positive reasons to spread the word about your firm.

8. You must be committed to achieving success. Have a vision, create plans and objectives and see them through to their conclusion. Consider each rejection or setback an opportunity to learn, grow and adapt your approach accordingly.

9. It is difficult to achieve a respectable degree of company success when working alone. You must command a crew to scale up to the "six-figure" level. Using your staff's time allows you to focus on expanding your business instead of being bogged down with mundane tasks.

In many regions, lawn care is seasonal, with a brief off-season during the winter. Learn how to take advantage of the off-season by offering your clients other services during the winter. Determine the optimal timing to launch your marketing initiatives so that your message reaches individuals at the end of the off-season, when they may be searching for a new lawn care provider.

Establishing an environmentally friendly lawn care provider can separate your business from the competition. Some astute owners of lawn mowing businesses are starting to advertise themselves as "Green" lawn care firms, with "green" referring to more than just the color of the grass they cut.

Capture the 'Green' Specialty Market

People's willingness to pay a premium for this service is the greatest benefit for a lawn care business that targets this specialized market. Typically, wealthy households support environmental initiatives.

Even if they are not truly concerned, they want their friends and neighbors to believe they are. Having your vehicle parked outside with your 'carbon neutral' lawn service logo prominently displayed is a terrific approach for a family to show that they care about the environment.

Equipment Friendly to the Environment

Using electric equipment rather than equipment that is fueled by fossil fuels is one approach to be more environmentally friendly. The problem with electric equipment is that it must be recharged, which might be problematic while traveling. Some lawn mowing service providers have installed solar panels on their trucks as an innovative solution to this issue.

Electric lawnmowers, edgers, blowers, and other lawn and garden tools are now available. They provide solutions that are both quieter and emit fewer pollutants. Some landscaping companies also utilize equipment powered by bio diesel.

Water Efficiency

A component of caring for the environment is water conservation. As a result of shifting views, lawn care companies now provide irrigation options that use significantly less water than in the past. Before installing an irrigation system, consumers will likely want to know how much water the system will use and if water consumption may be avoided.

Natural Fertilization

Other lawn care and landscaping companies are adopting an eco-friendly strategy by utilizing organic fertilizers. These 100% organic fertilizers can be more expensive and less effective than their synthetic counterparts. To minimize disappointment, consulting clients on what they can expect from organic fertilizers is essential.

Collaborate with other environmentally conscious businesses

Lawn care providers can improve their 'green' and 'clean' image by collaborating with other environmentally minded businesses. Collaboration with a company that installs solar panels is one example.

If you wish to be completely carbon neutral, you can need to offset the carbon emissions from your automobiles by purchasing carbon credits from an organization such as Carbonfund.org.

There will always be clients willing to pay a premium for this specialized service, so lawn care businesses that position themselves to capitalize on this niche will perform well over the long term. It is easier to earn a six-figure income from your lawn care business within two years if you take the time to learn how to work smarter instead of working harder.

CHAPTER 23

EVENT PLANNING OR PARTY PLANNING SERVICES

S tarting a party planning business from scratch is not always challenging. Upon reflection, no technical skills are required; everything relies on ingenuity and common sense.

No, neither a marketing degree nor the commercial understanding of a capitalist is required. You only need a vision, the honesty to assist others and the resolve in confronting obstacles head-on.

What is your goal?

What comes to mind about the "average" party planner?

Do you imagine a gregarious, outgoing person wearing a fashionable outfit and charming prospective clients with her brilliant smile and presentation skills?

Do you picture a man with a phone in a home office surrounded by organized folders?

Our perception of how party planners should dress and conduct themselves mirrors the nature of the party planning company we are launching.

Knowing Your Key to the Industry is the secret to a successful event planning firm.

You must be honest and identify whatever aspect of the entire process you excel at. Once you've recognized your greatest strength, you can construct your event-planning business around it!

You can start your self-analysis by recalling your child-hood. If you're like most people, you undoubtedly have fond recollections of setting up a soda store (or play business) with your pals, staffing it and feeling so darn accomplished at the end of the day.

Party planning is comparable to your first commercial venture as a child. You had an idea, a product or service to sell, and a team and you had to divide your responsibilities.

Now, in what aspect of your lemonade business did you excel? Were you the one greeting them with a smile in front of the store? You determined how the lemonade should taste, correct?

Studying the histories of successful party entrepreneurs reveals that they all began in a small sector of the party-organizing market. Those with culinary skills become caterers.

Those with interpersonal abilities became public relations consultants and event hosts. Those with expansive back-yards became the event hosts. Those with artistic ability became party goods sellers, table skirts and photographers.

The party business welcomes those willing to contribute and continue to develop. When you gain experience, you will also be able to identify your shortcomings and the aspects of party planning where you need to allocate more funds.

An introverted genius at money allocation may not be the ideal event host but he can always pay someone else to host the event. His forte is budgeting, which is also a significant requirement in this profession.

When you know what you can give to your communi-ty of party planners, you are one step closer to becoming the well-rounded party planner you've always envisioned yourself to be. Observe how people conduct themselves with your eyes wide open. True party entrepreneurs are not ashamed to admit their ignorance. They will continue to learn and grow while having a great time.

A business party may appear to be an oxymoron. While people typically equate parties with enjoyment, we tend to view work as "anti-fun." There are moments, though, when the two worlds collide: during a corporate party.

When arranging a party, it is helpful to be strictly business-oriented so that the party is strictly enjoyable. Here are some suggestions for making the event as enjoyable and productive as possible:

1. Choose a theme

Unfortunately, the "theme" of most business dinners is a meal at a luxury restaurant, followed by a return home. Although such a dinner is "strictly business," it is certainly not enjoyable.

Choosing a theme for a corporate party can add flavor. Employees will enjoy the event more if it has a theme, likely boosting their view of the workplace. These are some popular themes for business parties:

Casino Hollywood Luau Mardi Gras Paris Classic Western

Such topics will help employees temporarily escape the business environment and enter the "real world."

2. Combine a holiday party and an awards presentation.

Typically, while arranging a business holiday party, the question is how to include business in the event. One option is to use the occasion to award various staff.

This helps to "legitimize" the event and eliminates the perception that employees are required to attend business parties for the sake of office politics. Adding an awards ceremony to the event will increase employee motivation to attend.

3. Limit your intake of sweets

According to conventional thinking, a successful party planning firm must include smaller desserts. At business meals, full-size dessert dishes are rarely consumed. Consider establishing a dessert station with smaller serving sizes. This will help people with a sweet tooth while reducing food waste. It is an excellent business concept!

4. Dress casually to save money

If you want to reduce the expense of a party, you can do it indirectly by maintaining a "business casual" dress code for party planners. Essentially, this relates to anticipations. When guests are dressed formally, they won't anticipate pizza and Coke.

The visitors won't anticipate caviar and you won't faint when you receive the bill if you make the party "business casual." Remember that you don't need to spend a fortune to throw a successful corporate party.

5. Restrict or ban alcoholic beverages

Eliminating them can prevent future liabilities. You have viable alternative possibilities, however. You can limit the number of alcoholic beverages to two. Another alternative is to limit accessible beverages to beer and wine. A further alternative is to provide guests with a single beverage kind. These solutions will ultimately minimize the party's expenses.

Yes, parties and businesses can coexist. In reality, these events can improve cooperation and friendship in any industry. These business party planning tips will make your event completely business but more importantly, strictly enjoyable!

CHAPTER 24

RESUME WRITING SERVICES

R esumes are often described as the first step in obtaining an interview. To put it broadly, a solid, well-documented résumé may do wonders for your career. As a result, resume writing has become a business in the modern era. Who wouldn't want to make a favorable first impression? Therefore, a strong resume is advantageous.

It is a reality that most job seekers in the current climate lack the power of an ideal combination. We are strictly discussing a person's curriculum vitae and it is not unnatural for a person with fewer abilities but a very prestigious and shining CV to be able to sway an employer.

Generally, it has been observed that most job seekers make a few significant mistakes regarding a potential company. These individuals believe that an employer has divine ability to distinguish between qualified and unqualified candidates.

This is a complete farce, as the businesses in issue receive hundreds of job bio data for a single position daily, making it nearly impossible to differentiate between each candidate. A resume with an advantage over its competitors will undoubtedly be successful; therefore, it must be completed flawlessly.

It has been observed that a candidate with a more professionally crafted resume is considerably more qualified for a certain position than the competition. This may signal disappointment for the more qualified candidates but such is the way the cookie crumbles.

Communication is essential and those who achieve success are superior communicators. We are primarily discussing communicating via a resume. One must remember that the better one's resume, the greater one's chances of passing an interview and landing the job.

Logically, all potential employers would want to see your CV and this basic document will influence your chances of landing the job. When it comes to a proper job interview, those mentioned above "humiliating piece of paper" plays an omnipotent role. As such, it is a small item that deserves much attention and reverence. It should be considered with the highest care and significance since it can make or ruin a career.

Indeed, having an impressive resume is the first step to success and serves as your introduction to the company. To obtain an interview, you must have a job biodata that is impressive and produced professionally.

A well-crafted resume improves the situation and facilitates your journey to your chosen position. Therefore, it is best to maintain an impressively written resume, as this will serve you well. It is not surprising that job searchers constantly search for resume writing services to strengthen their CVs.

A resume writing service is an excellent method to make supplemental income or, even better, to launch a full-time enterprise. A resume is a sort of document that summarizes a candidate's qualifications and experience for employment purposes.

Strong writing skills can considerably improve the client's chances of landing the desired position. Here are methods for launching a resume writing service.

Purpose of a Resume Writing Service

* Clients seeking jobs occasionally can't find the time to construct resumes. This is where the service comes in to fulfill their employment criteria.

Also, you can provide value by offering to create cover letters and referral letters for clients who request them.

Before developing a CV, you can advertise your services through various channels, such as fliers, newspapers and personal websites shared on social networking sites such as Facebook.

Possessions of a Resume Writing Service

* Effective writing skills make the resume, cover letter, etc., significantly more persuasive and appealing to the company.

A place to store your office supplies, such as high-quality paper and a sturdy printer, is essential. In addition, a computer with a broadband Internet connection is required to maintain contact with clients for other information.

Many factors to consider

* Before starting a resume writing business, you must invest in equipment and promotion. Your investment will ultimately be profitable due to the resume-writing business's medium to a large market size. Applicants continuously seek employment, so you should never be concerned about losing potential customers.

Always be understanding and patient with your clients. Consider those clients that require constant updates on the work's progress. Inconvenient as it may be, it is essential to keep clients informed about the project you are currently working on.

* Choose between full-time and part-time employment to avoid dissatisfied clients. Not delivering the expected output could result in negative feedback.

First, you can find that writing resumes, cover letters, etc., can be time-consuming but as you gain experience, the work will become significantly more efficient.

* Always remember that writing is a hobby, not a job, to reduce stress.

CHAPTER 25

TRANSCRIPTION OR DATA ENTRY SERVICES

Have you seen all the advertisements for data entry or typing from home? The negative aspect of these advertisements is that they are not recruiting you. They are offering information that provides a list of purportedly hiring organizations.

Often, this list is inaccurate and lists companies attempting to sell you their items for more money. You eventually give up out of frustration that you had wasted your time and are no closer to earning extra money at home than when you began.

This section won't provide a list of organizations that are hiring. Instead, we will examine the skills a data entry worker must possess to get employed. To identify hiring organizations, you should visit TJobs.com and click on the data entry option.

Computers have changed how businesses file information. Almost everything is stored online and must be attributed to someone. They don't wish to hire full-time workers who require compensation and benefits. They choose to outsource this labor, which presents a chance for those who can type to work from home.

So, are you an expert computer user? It will be necessary to utilize spreadsheets and word-processing software. You must be able to utilize software applications.

Data entry tasks can range from medical transcription to database entry of names and addresses. Regardless of the type of data entry you perform, you can do it from home, which offers many advantages.

A data entry operator generates lists of names, phone numbers and addresses. The data is subsequently entered into forms that appear on the computer screen. Are you detail-oriented? You can be requested to revise and proofread existing content.

Word processing entails writing letters and reports. Many firms may give a template for all documents to be processed to make your life easier and ensure that you deliver the consistent service they seek.

Here are some suggestions for starting a home-based data entry business. If you prefer this type of employment, your options are virtually limitless. You won't become wealthy but you can earn a decent life while being at home. This advantage makes it a highly desirable business to enter.

Transcription and data entry is often the first two tasks that come to mind when individuals consider telecommuting. There are a few parallels between the occupations:

- A quick typing speed (60 WPM or better)
- Accurate keystrokes
- Reliable computer
- Trustworthy internet connection (probably high speed)

Despite their similarities, the jobs are significantly distinct.

Transcription positions necessitate further training, particularly when transcribing audio recordings. Transcriptions in the medical and legal fields are substantially more specialized.

It may also necessitate the procurement of a four-track stenographer. A strong vocabulary and command of grammar are also essential. The standard pay scale for transcription is from $0.06 to $0.12 per line.

Freelance transcriptionists can receive steady employment from multiple companies. However, there are instances in which individuals can obtain full-time work with benefits at a single organization. If you already have an office-based transcription position, proposing telecommuting to your company may be worthwhile.

Less specialized data entry jobs can be similarly demanding. Typing accuracy is of the utmost importance, not just with the regular keyboard but also with the ten key. First, data entry positions may pay an average of $8 per hour. There is considerable rivalry for the data entry position.

After deciding whether the career suits you, you must determine whether you want to approach it as an employee or as a business owner giving your skills freelance. Both approaches have advantages and disadvantages.

If you own and operate your firm, you can choose your jobs, schedule and vacation time. However, you must also keep track of your income and expenses for tax purposes. You are spared the other paperwork associated with owning your firm if you are an employee.

To maintain a positive working relationship with the businesses you interact with daily, you must conduct yourself professionally.

CHAPTER 26

VIRTUAL ASSISTANT SERVICES

A re you interested in launching a virtual assistant business? You've arrived at the correct location. As more businesses continue to do transactions online, virtual assistants are becoming increasingly in demand. Virtual assistants (or VAs) operate remotely from their client's offices. Rarely, if ever, does a virtual assistant visit the workplace of the client he or she serves.

A VA does different tasks, such as answering telephone calls, updating websites, replying to e-mails, transcribing transcripts, writing articles and performing light bookkeeping. The duties of a VA rely mostly on the demands of the clients and the VA's specialty or area of expertise.

Who Employs Virtual Assistants?

Small business owners, particularly those with online operations, are the typical clients of virtual assistants. Virtual assistants aid these small business owners by reducing their workload, allowing them to devote their time and energy to revenue-generating activities rather than administrative responsibilities.

However, online business owners are not the only ones who employ VAs. Some businesses engage virtual assistants rather than real staff to do administrative duties. VAs are more cost-effective for these businesses because they work remotely with their equipment and file taxes. VAs are, therefore, independent contractors.

Today, the need for VAs is extremely high. You can start your own VA firm with basic office skills and excellent organizational abilities. A virtual assistant business may be your ideal if you have earlier worked in an administrative role.

If you decide to establish your virtual assistant (VA) firm, remember that you can work for multiple clients simultaneously; therefore, you must have excellent time management abilities.

How to Establish a Virtual Assistant Enterprise

So let me respond to your inquiry regarding how to launch a virtual assistant business. To start a VA business, you need a computer, a fast Internet connection, an e-mail address, office applications software (e.g., word processing, spreadsheet, accounting, etc.), a phone, a fax machine, a printer, a scanner and, of course, a website. Also, you will need a desk, chair and workspace.

Set up your home office before promoting your virtual assistant website. There are methods for promoting your new business. You can advertise on websites and e-zines, employ pay-per-click advertising, contact potential customers via e-mail and participate in online discussion groups and forums. You can offer first-time customers discounted pricing.

Once your virtual assistant service is up and running and you have one or two clients, don't hesitate to ask for references. Clients satisfied with your service are often eager to recommend you to others needing a virtual assistant.

This is an ideal time for administratively skilled individuals who aspire to become self-employed in this extremely in-demand business. It will not be simple but anyone who wants to can establish a virtual assistant business with sufficient research materials and effort.

The current economic climate has compelled many businesses to cut costs and personnel. This doesn't mean that the task is no longer necessary. The big question business owners raise when presented with this predicament is "How am I meant to conduct my business and look after everything else simultaneously?" Employing a virtual assistant is the finest solution.

It might be overbearing if a person is serious about becoming a VA and pursuing self-employment. Conduct research, enroll in classes, attend workshops, network with other VAs, join online communities and take copious notes.

A virtual assistant is an independent business owner who provides a service to other business owners. When your clients are successful, so are you! It's a win-win situation for all parties involved."

CHAPTER 27

GRAPHIC DESIGN OR WEB DESIGN SERVICES

C reativity and innovation are intertwined; in this realm of creativity, wild imaginations and new revolutionary ideas keep the ball going. Everyone, from aspiring designers to seasoned professionals, has the opportunity to showcase their talents and earn money.

To learn how to make a living through graphic design online and generate money, you must grasp how it works.

It is essential to remember that the online and offline design market is highly competitive, but there is also a great demand for excellent designers. Online graphic design has vast potential.

You can create T-shirts, mugs, caps, jeans, websites, blogs, flash presentations, templates, logos, business cards, icons and calendars. The list is endless, as are the possibilities.

To obtain information on how to earn money online through graphic design, visiting different websites that provide such services online is necessary. Join websites that sell stock images to get started. You can post your visual samples here.

You can sell graphic illustrations and vector files on these websites. You can select your assignments. Consider joining these sites only as a stepping stone, as they may not yield exceptionally high earnings but they provide a great platform for showcasing your work and gaining recognition.

Once you're accustomed to the task and feel comfortable, investigate how to earn money online by designing websites, themes, templates for blogs and forums, logos, movies, etc. These initiatives will yield greater earnings than uploading your work on stock image services.

Sell your work through membership-only websites. A list of loyal members will generate recurring revenue. Online prospects for freelance graphic designers are abundant and they are compensated well for good work.

Remember that joining multiple websites and showcasing your work won't generate sufficient income and employment. You must consistently produce high-quality work and advertise yourself effectively.

Place samples of your work on social networking sites and below email signatures in online discussion forums in which you engage. Create a network of individuals who enjoy your job, as they are the ones who will continue to hire you.

Establish your internet shop. This will allow you to maximize your abilities and internet resources. Remember that competition in this field is fierce. Some people make a living from Graphic Designing and Web Designing by working online and make a respectable living doing so.

As with any commercial endeavor, starting a web design business involves careful planning. Which area of Web design do you wish to emphasize? The accessible niches include graphic design, interior design, web development and web hosting, to name a few. Feel free to examine the other niches to locate a suitable fit.

After deciding on a niche, you must conduct an extensive study by creating a business strategy. You must examine web design from multiple perspectives, including the opportunities it brings and how your abilities and shortcomings fit into the grand scheme. Experience is advantageous in this field but lack of experience should not dissuade you.

Many resources can assist you in increasing your level of experience. You can compensate for your lack of expertise by forming a partnership with an expert in the field or you can choose to hire more skilled personnel. You can gain the necessary skills by attending a course or teaching yourself.

Your business plan must also include problems such as your financial projections for the upcoming year and, preferably, for the subsequent five years, an analysis of what your competitors are doing and how you will position yourself to function successfully regardless of the competition.

A business plan must be a living document that guides you from point A, the decision to establish a web design firm, to point B, the actual launch and operation of the business.

After successfully drafting your business plan and acquiring adequate finances, you must assemble the necessary equipment to operate your business. This includes a computer and different software packages. Since this is a dynamic and constantly evolving area, I recommend conducting internet research on the most popular items in use.

Before making a financial commitment, you should research product reviews to make an educated decision. Start with the bare least you can get away with while still providing your clients competent service. As your business and experience expand, you can add more service-enhancing packages to your toolkit.

After successfully establishing and operating your firm, you must promote it so potential customers can locate you. You can promote your business offline or online, although the latter method is less expensive and yields faster results. Business promotion is a skill in and of itself. If not done correctly, your business will suffer.

If you have sufficient cash, you can choose to outsource this very essential duty or you can learn to do it yourself. I prefer the second choice since no one knows your business and you do, nor will they be as enthusiastic. Check out the resources listed below if you want to acquire the marketing skills necessary for the success of your business.

CHAPTER 28

TRANSLATION SERVICES

In the global marketplace of the present day, the demand for professional translation services continues to rise. Historically, this service was mostly utilized by government leaders during significant political conferences and meetings.

Today, translations are required by a wide range of individuals for a vast array of purposes. Consequently, they are now integral to every business and government service. Every day, a wide diversity of individuals and languages require translation and interpretation services of the highest quality.

Translation services help individuals function in a multicultural society and play a vital role in preserving and promoting the richness and beauty of worldwide languages. In every element of life, the ability to communicate and be understood is vital. Therefore, a translator is required wherever one or more international languages are spoken.

Translation services are not limited to converting texts from one language to another. They are highly professional services, accustomed to handling sensitive and secret material and capable of translating highly technical phrases such as financial, medical, scientific and technological terminology. Even routine corporate documentation can become fairly complex, requiring a great linguist to interpret it effectively.

For instance, the medical field must be able to converse with foreign nationals who may require treatment in the United States. Their English proficiency may not be sufficient to read and manage medical forms, drugs and prescriptions completely.

Similarly, in the legal profession, court proceedings and police matters, precise translation and interpretation are required to guarantee that all parties comprehend the information being delivered. These are some areas in which professional translation services are essential to the health and protection of human rights.

The possibility that a business has worldwide clients or consumers is substantial, particularly in the global economy of the present day. Naturally, no company wants to miss out on the chance to conduct business on a global scale. Therefore, the need for proper translation comes to the forefront.

A straightforward order confirmation may need to be translated for an overseas buyer to read and comprehend it. Likewise, non-bilingual businesspeople in this country will need their international correspondence translated into English.

The services of a translation or interpreter would help any individual organization or enterprise. Recent industry figures indicate that the requirement for internet firms to provide translations of their website content and online interactions has grown significantly over the past two to three years.

This tendency is anticipated to continue. The vast majority of trustworthy translation services provide various languages and language combinations.

In addition to the common European languages such as French, German, Dutch, Spanish, Polish and Italian, they will also provide Ukrainian, Urdu, Hindi, Mandarin, Japanese, Russian, Arabic and Hebrew, among others and most professional translators are linguists in more than two languages, capable of translating in a range of combinations, such as Russian to English and Japanese and vice versa.

The demand for translation services will expand as our nation becomes more culturally diverse and as a result of the effects of globalization on our economy.

Most, if not all, of the world's largest firms provide Spanish translations of their IVR systems, marketing literature and other custom promotional things. This is simple for them to achieve because they have the budget and staff to devote to it but this is not the case for small business owners, which is where you come in!

Consider starting a Translation Service business if you are proficient in many languages. This is a very marketable ability. The Internet has had a significant impact on marketing over the past 15 years; for the first time in history, a small business owner can reach a global audience with only a few mouse clicks.

Unfortunately, most don't take advantage of this amazing opportunity because they fear language and cultural difficulties. If a Translation Service sounds like a business in which you might be interested, consider the following:

The need for professional translation services has increased among corporations and individuals in recent years. Globalization has unmistakably signified that both large and small businesses are attempting to reach the global market and are therefore expanding via their websites and legal contracts; because these websites and legal contracts are written exclusively in the native language, it is quite difficult for specialists from other countries or provinces to comprehend them. Due to these factors, only translation services have experienced a significant increase.

To translate or have something translated into a foreign language such as French, Italian or Spanish is a laborious endeavor that one should only do once or twice. Eventually, though, it gets rather burdensome and the person considers giving up. Multiple websites have begun offering translation services to their consumers in response to this issue.

Websites offer corporate translation services for papers, reports, brochures, etc., brief translation services for blogs, multilingual FAQs, etc., and writing and rewriting services. You can also request expert assistance for unique requirements such as website translation, DTP or page layout and the creation of multilingual documents.

Entering overseas markets can bring any business greater profitability and faster growth than the domestic market. As most organizations must display their websites in one international language and multiple other languages, translation services can greatly assist. In such situations, online language translation services can be useful.

How everything becomes actualized

It is essential to comprehend how corporations and translators operate. Certified individuals hired by the companies translate the languages. If a company solely focuses on the German market, it will employ a specialist who can translate the local language into German and vice versa.

When this process of translating the writing is complete, the software professionals localize the programs and do localization testing. Thus, websites are translated while the original format is also preserved.

Language has enormous importance in the modern world. This is a medium for transmitting information from one location to another. Some businesses even outsource the creation of their websites, brochures, etc and have them translated to expand their products and services to international markets by making the information accessible to everybody. This is why most businesses employ language professionals to' create their official documents.'

They desire higher levels of professionalism in the translation, as it will be shown to customers. Therefore, websites offer translation services for nearly every language in the world.

They maintain the same level of professionalism when translating the content and serve you according to your specifications. They know that your ultimate goal in employing them is to obtain a competitive edge in the global market.

CHAPTER 29

PERSONAL TRAINING OR FITNESS COACHING SERVICES

Perhaps you are considering a career as a fitness instructor. I adore it and it's what I've been doing for years, with the double benefit that I've been able to exercise and make money while helping others work out their bodies! Oh right, sweetie, feel the fire!

Since this is possible for you, I recommend you investigate becoming an online fitness coach. Now, this can significantly twist the grey matter of yourr cerebrum cortex upon first hearing it; thus, slowly read and digest what I am stating.

A minuscule minority of health and fitness organizations are evaluating unique and creative business models that construct enormous online communities where individuals may learn about fitness and receive feedback from online resources, experts and personal online fitness coaches.

You and your quest to become a fitness instructor are a wonderful fit for this groundbreaking new business model and you can do it part-time from your computer!

Think Outside The Box: Ever since the internet has come along the conventional ways of doing business is changing worldwide. Also occurring in our industry of health and fitness!

If you are seeking to become a fitness instructor or are already one, consider what many others are doing in addition to their main job since it keeps you in the field with the possibility to earn a substantial amount of extra money while helping people with a game-changing chance.

Sadly, relatively few fitness instructors, personal trainers and health/nutrition professionals will be aware of this business concept.

Simply put, you are regarded as a personal coach. As a personal coach, you DON'T require any special training or certification. You are a source of direction, guidance, inspiration and a model for many individuals seeking to improve their health.

You are self-employed and can earn rising residual income because you are passionate about fitness and health and enjoy assisting others!

If you truly desire to become a fitness instructor, you should pursue this goal. However, I will exaggerate my enthusiasm for you to comprehend what is going on with this highly potent new business model for health and fitness enthusiasts who don't mind making much money along the way.

Every individual who launches a personal training business does so to achieve success. Others desire the independence of working for themselves, whereas some are motivated by the prospect of achieving substantial financial success via fitness. The bottom line is that success is the primary objective.

Unfortunately, not everyone who starts a fitness business to achieve success is ultimately successful. In reality, most people don't achieve great success. Why? Because they lack the right personal trainer education.

There are three pillars of personal training company success that any professional trainer who aspires to the top must adhere to. If you neglect one of the three pillars of fitness business success, your results will be compromised.

Suppose you are truly committed to dominating your niche in the personal trainer business market. In that case, I urge you to implement not one, wo but all three of the fitness pro success pillars outlined below. Every successful professional possesses all three qualities.

Three Pillars of Personal Training Business Success

1. Continuing education for personal trainers

Never believe that you know everything there is to know about exercise science. As the industry continues to evolve, you must remain at the forefront by being abreast of current events. Learn as much as can about anatomy, exercise physiology, kinesiology and nutrition.

Spending a predetermined amount of time and money each week on continuing education is prudent. Participate in fitness industry seminars and workshops. Ensure that you receive monthly research papers from NSCA and/or ACSM.

View videos and read the blogs of the industry's most esteemed strength and conditioning professionals. With the introduction of the Internet, continuing education for your training business has become pretty straightforward. You have immediate access to the necessary information.

Commit to investing in your trainer education indefinitely. The most effective fitness professionals place a premium on continuing education.

2. Examine the marketing and sales of personal trainers

If you want a good wage in the fitness industry, you must first learn how to attract and sell clients. Without this ability, you could be the best fitness trainer in the world but nobody would know it.

Invest a quarter of the time you invest in the physical training portion of your business towards learning how to sell and advertise personal fitness training. This action will undoubtedly propel your business to the next level.

You should often attend personal trainer business seminars, invest in fitness business courses and subscribe to online personal training business periodicals like Personal Training Insider.

3. Continuous investigation of human behavior and fitness training

The three pillars of personal training business success are educating yourself on coaching, motivating and influencing others. As a professional fitness trainer, isn't it your responsibility?

Motivate and influence health and fitness improvement. If you want to have a significant impact on people's lives, you must continually invest in the study of human behavior. Remember that you are in an industry where you must motivate others to act.

The most effective personal trainers adhere to the three business pillars described above. To succeed as a fitness trainer, you must continue investing in your education.

CHAPTER 30

MUSICAL INSTRUCTION AND INSTRUMENT RENTALS

Private music teachers teach a single instrument, typically one-on-one or in small groups. Often, these classes take place at the homes of the teacher or the student or they may take place in a school setting, with the student leaving a larger class to spend time with the teacher.

In a private studio or a school, the parent pays the teacher "per lesson" for this type of music session and this section aims to boost the income of these teachers. This section outlines four ways to boost revenue as a private music teacher; some may not be ideal for all teachers but hopefully, they provide insight into how private music teachers might increase their earnings.

1. Never refund or credit a lesson since it is in the client's best interest.

Students miss lessons. This is a fact. People become sick, there are special sporting events and there are occasions when students will miss their music session for whatever reason. The reality is that this can't be avoided.

As a music instructor, you can establish a policy stating, "lessons are always made up; they are never refunded or credited to your account." However, the WHY behind this statement is often overlooked; it should be because it is essential for the student's advancement on their instrument.

If you adhere to this concept, you will never have to battle with parents since it is in the best interest of the pupils, not yours. If you start the arrangement with this agreement in place, you will have a lot easier time enforcing it; the parents will make an effort to make up the lesson instead of you having to urge it. Having student outcomes (such as an assessment or exam) in place makes it even simpler to ensure they occur.

You will need to create time to make up the lessons; it may be necessary to set aside one or two days during the holidays or non-contact time; nevertheless, the ability to do so will be well worth the extra cash it generates. Often, the parents won't pay and you won't have to credit or return any money!

2. Identify your niche and establish exclusivity in that niche.

If you have something unique to offer in your teaching, you will attract more and higher-quality students and be able to charge more.

For instance, suppose you teach guitar. If you teach everyone who shows up, you will likely have small children, adolescents and possibly one or two adults and you will have to teach a range of genres based on the type of music the students want.

If, on the other hand, you develop a niche business specializing in only one field, people will eventually seek you out since you are a specialist and you'll be able to charge more for your services and only accept the students you want.

Examples of guitar specialty businesses include: - a business that specializes in guitars for young children; - a business that helps adults realize their ambitions of playing guitar in a band, and - a business that specializes in heavy metal guitar.

These are merely examples; there are tens of thousands of potential niches. However, the niche must be something buyers genuinely want; it can't be something you think is nice.

3. Increase your retention rate and don't accept every student as a student.

Increasing your retention rate is essential for all businesses but especially for music teachers, whose income is dependent on the number of students they teach multiplied by the amount they charge per student. If you improve the quality and standard of the kids you teach while reducing the number of students you lose, you will slowly grow your income and have a more fulfilling teaching role daily.

You should not accept every student that applies for admission. You should always meet and interview new students before agreeing to teach them, as they may not be as reliable as your regular students in paying their fees and attending lessons.

By avoiding "difficult" students in the first place, you will be able to concentrate on more productive activities and pupils of a higher caliber, which will undoubtedly boost your earning potential.

Most retention issues may be linked to one factor: pupils' lack of motivation due to insufficient practice. The fun music company instructors' blog has retention-enhancing tactics, including practice systems and ideas for making courses more enjoyable.

4. Add passive income streams to your firm as the fourth strategy.

Income from teaching is active income; if you quit teaching, your income ceases. This is acceptable, as it is comparable to any earned income. You should also seek to include passive income in your business.

Do you create instructional materials for use in music classes or lessons?

If so, you are ideally situated to add passive income to your income mix. Simply publish your materials so that your students and others can view them. It might be as simple as having the materials printed and bound exclusively for your pupils at a copy shop.

Do you purchase and distribute books and music to your students?

If so, you can negotiate bulk reductions with suppliers and charge students the full retail price of the books. Parents will appreciate not having to visit a store to purchase the books if you sell them through your company.

Can you sell leads to other businesses or teachers?

For example, each student must acquire an instrument. If you suggest your students to a music store to purchase their instruments, it is occasionally feasible to receive a commission. Using affiliate schemes is undoubtedly doable on the Internet.

CHAPTER 31

CAR DETAILING

There are three ways to start a car detailing business: the Mobile way, the Expressway and the Site-based approach. The mobile business is the quickest and most convenient way to launch a Car Detailing (CD) service and many customers like to have their vehicles detailed in front of their eyes.

It is also the business that requires the smallest first investment of $2,000 or less. However, it demands a lot of stamina, patience, and the ability to travel to the client's location to complete your commitments under trying situations.

You must perform exterior detailing on the vehicles, including washing, waxing and polishing. You must also perform interior detailing, such as removing stains from the upholstery, vacuuming the carpets and cleaning the various floor mats.

Also, you must polish and shine the wheels and tires. CD-specific items are the most critical information you must have for success. You should know the paint, finish and upholstery types for each effective and safe product.

Express Auto Detailing is also a lucrative company, so you can consider starting a CD service at any car wash or auto dealership. You can also establish partnerships with hotels that offer concierge services, auto shows, limousine services, RV shops, gas stations, etc. All these locations provide substantial client potential and can generate consistent revenue.

The Express Car Detailing services are gaining popularity among consumers who can't afford the complete auto detailing service or who can't leave their vehicle for many hours. These consumers appreciate having a car that is both aesthetically appealing and protected from the elements.

Many automatic car wash firms offer this service, in which the vehicle is cleaned, dried and machine-waxed to provide approximately three months of protection. Customers can also receive speedy interior detailing and express carpet detailing services.

The purpose of providing consumers with "Express Auto Detailing" is to provide a quick-fix solution in a quick amount of time. The website-based CD business is legitimate. Starting a CD business requires a substantial investment. It is a free service that is also the most profitable of all. You can do many services simultaneously and so earn more.

In this business, the customer leaves his vehicle in your care and returns at the specified time to retrieve it. You can offer your customers different detailing options. You can start your auto detailing service if you have the financial resources and a conveniently situated location to launch a full-fledged CD business.

How to Obtain Your First Customers

The challenge for new vehicle detailing firms is that they lack a reliable resource for acquiring new consumers. They don't comprehend that they have fast, free access to most people selling cars in their city. Where is this location? Craigslist.

Craigslist is now the busiest marketplace in the world for selling secondhand vehicles. There is a vast inventory of automobiles for sale by owners and dealers and it is free and simple to search. There is also a highly visited automotive services section on Craigslist.

If you post a professional-looking ad presenting yourself, your services and your costs, you will receive phone calls and e-mails. You must present detailed justifications for why your auto detailing service is superior to others on Craigslist.

There, most detailers highlight their low pricing. However, this strategy is faulty. The difficulty with selling just on pricing is that the buyer believes the quality of your job to be worse.

Instead, stress your service's quality. Describe in detail your detailed procedure. Provide a summary of your professional detailing experience. Specify the equipment and goods you own and utilize.

And if you have photographs of your work, showcasing them is persuasive. Don't only display photographs of your completed job. Instead, provide before-and-after images of common problems, such as dirty interiors and rusted paint, for which a person selling a car is seeking professional assistance.

Car dealers will also contact you, as they spend a significant amount of time daily on Craigslist. Although you cannot desire all their business, some excellent auto dealers offer competitive rates and consistent sales. It is usually beneficial to have a steady source of monthly revenue to cover expenses.

Therefore, if you are a new auto detailing firm seeking more employment, you should publish as many Craigslist ads as possible. Examine the Craigslist advertisements of your competitors to determine how you might improve their message and attract more customers.

Often, all that is required is a more professional presentation with other information and images of your services. You will find that many consumers are searching for a more reliable auto detailer than the lowest alternative on Craigslist.

CHAPTER 32

MOBILE CAR WASH SERVICES

How do small mobile car washing and detailing services to get their start? If this is truly what you want to accomplish, I will offer you the information and encouragement you need to complete this on your own and briefly share my experience. However, I must warn you: It is Extremely Difficult!

Consider undertaking other fleet washing contracts.

When I started my mobile car wash business in the early 1980s, there was no competition. Certain individuals offered mobile auto detailing services, but there was no infrastructure for washing huge vehicles in parking lots.

Now, a few companies went to auto dealerships to spray off the vehicles but that is not comparable to the full wash, soap and dry, and vacuum services that mobile car washes provide today.

Fortunately, as one of the very first individuals in the field, our business grew rapidly because there were so many automobiles. As we began to view the business as more of a production process than a pure service business, we began to examine faster methods for washing vehicles.

First, we established that the most efficient approach to washing a large number of vehicles was to line them up in rows. Typically, the vehicles lined up in rows are fleets belonging to government organizations or huge services.

Then there were the smaller fleets, such as pizza delivery services, auto parts delivery companies and small service organizations with small fleets. Recently, someone asked me an essential question regarding the mobile vehicle washing industry.

What strategies would you recommend for acquiring fleet accounts?

First, I suggest putting together a copy of your liability insurance, followed by a one-page sales letter and a compact brochure that may be customized based on the fleet type, pricing and number of cars.

Second, speaking with the person in charge of the company's fleets makes sense. If it is a government agency, you must register on a bidders list and wait until they send out solicitations.

Due to the recession's end, many businesses and government organizations are attempting to cut costs. They are all tightening their belts to maintain efficiency; therefore, you must sharpen your pencil and give a low-cost, high-volume business at costs that are commensurate with this. Due to incredibly tight budgets, layoffs and major cost reductions, they may be extremely tardy to pay their invoices.

In addition, I urge that you explain your high level of customer service and guarantee that you will always be fair to them. In other words, if a customer ever complains, you will swiftly respond and rectify the problem. One of the issues with mobile vehicle wash companies and mobile truck fleet cleaning services is that they do a poor job and are often late.

They often bill for services that were never provided. You must demonstrate to businesses and government organizations that you are not a "fly-by-night" company and will follow through on your commitments. Please consider the following.

Marketing

A mobile car wash company is one of the easiest companies to launch. Of all, starting a business is not difficult, especially one like this that has no inventory can be run by a single person with no employees and requires no physical location.

The trick is to locate customers. I know what you're thinking: that acquiring consumers for a mobile car wash service is a topic unworthy of an article because everyone owns a car and the world is filthy. What are you saying right now?

"What the heck, my car is filthy; I'll be your first customer. Come on over, it's in the driveway and filthy and while you're at it, vacuum it!"

Indeed, acquiring car wash clients for a mobile automobile cleaning and washing service or even a mobile auto detailing business is relatively straightforward. Finding high-paying, persistent, loyal consumers who regularly suggest you to others is an altogether different matter.

To effectively market a mobile car wash business, you will need business cards and flyers and you will need to target the recipients of those flyers. Otherwise, you will find yourself driving all over town washing one or two cars at a time when you should be washing 10 to 20 cars in a row every week at office parks. You must carefully target your direct marketing campaigns and concentrate your clients in upmarket office parks.

CHAPTER 33

MOBILE HAIR AND MAKEUP SERVICES

A mobile beauty business can be incredibly profitable, especially because it doesn't have to pay for a physical location. However, there are other fees associated with launching a mobile beauty service.

In addition to tools, supplies and products, you will require marketing materials and insurance. In further depth, let's examine the costs associated with launching a mobile beauty business.

Equipment, Supplies and Goods

Whether you are a hairdresser, a makeup artist or provide other beauty services, you will require the proper equipment to do your duties efficiently. For instance, brushes, applicators and other specialized tools. Portable chairs, benches, towels and palettes may be required.

Create a list of all the items you need and conduct offline and online market research to determine the best deals. Consider both price and quality. You want your equipment to be safe and of sufficient quality.

Insurance

You want to secure adequate insurance to protect yourself and your clients in an accident. To administer treatments in someone's home, you must have professional indemnity insurance and public liability insurance, which protects you if a client files a claim against you.

Once more, conduct research and shop around for the greatest price. If you are located in the United Kingdom, the British Association of Beauty Therapy and Cosmetology (BABTAC) offers insurance packages to its members, often at subsidized rates.

To be successful as a wedding makeup artist, you must be adept at promoting yourself and your business. Here are five methods for spreading the word you can or may not have heard of.

Press Statements

Press releases are a cost-effective approach to marketing your business. Send at least one per month to local media to advertise your business. Include a compelling headline that piques the reader's interest (consider which headlines grab your attention!

You can send a press release to inform the public about the opening of your firm, the addition of a new product or service, your attendance at a particular event, your charitable activity and other important happenings.

Postal mailings (e.g., leaflet dropping)

Direct mailings are an excellent method for promoting your business locally. Create an advertisement on A5 paper or your business card and either distribute it yourself or engage a distribution company. If you have teenagers who need extra cash, this may also work!

Include a call to action in your advertisement or on your business card and utilize it to compile a list of prospective clients.

Distribute pamphlets and business cards to bridal advisors, bridal stores and caterers, hair salons, stylish boutiques and dress retailers.

Cross-Marketing

Cross-promotion is very useful for marketing a bridal make-up artistry business and involves presenting your services alongside those of another company. Is there, for instance, a wedding boutique prepared to market your services in exchange for your promotion of theirs?

You can cross-promote with a plastic surgeon or oncologist if you offer specialized cosmetics services for deformed clientele. Get acquainted with area events and party planners! Contact local vendors with whom you wish to do business.

Volunteer Work

Choose a charity and volunteer to do their cosmetics for free. Perhaps you could offer a night of pampering or a fashion show where you apply makeup to the models. You will become known and the charity is likely to spread your message. You can also share information about the occasion with a press release. Working with a charity can improve your standing in the community.

Fish dishes

If situated in a location frequented by your ideal clientele, a fishbowl can be quite profitable. It is merely a bowl or box in which you can collect business cards or provide a simple survey for individuals to complete in exchange for something of value, such as a drawing for a makeover. You can contact everyone who submits their information, winner or not, to inform them of your products and services.

To be perceived as an expert and a professional, investing in excellent business cards, client record cards and a high-quality website is worthwhile. Also, you will need a strong portfolio to demonstrate your abilities to potential clients.

Also, there will be ongoing expenses. As a mobile business, you won't have the significant overhead expenditures of a salon and personnel. Still, you will have expenses such as your car, telephone bill, replenishing the materials and items used in your business and some marketing initiatives.

The real cost of launching a mobile beauty business will vary based on the services offered to clients and the first investment made in equipment, supplies and goods. Understanding the costs of launching a mobile beauty business is essential to achieving the desired success.

CHAPTER 34

MOBILE MASSAGE THERAPY

Not only has the modern lifestyle promoted growth, professional satisfaction, entrepreneurship and advancements in many spheres but it has also raised performance-related stress, increasing the usefulness of alternative healing approaches such as massage therapy!

What has once primarily considered the domain of physiotherapists is now in high demand as a value-added service in spas, health farms and hotels, as people crave the relaxation and tranquility that a good massage therapist can provide with a spin of the fingers!

While it may not always be possible to rent huge and opulent-looking offices or commercial chambers for massage therapy business, one can start small by purchasing a van to offer mobile massage treatment packages that provide quality massages at low prices.

It is also a considerably lower investment than renting or purchasing a location and employing a large number of people with added overheads; also, having a mobile massage therapy business allows one to set their schedule, have a wider reach to customers, be self-employed and enjoy more freedom than massage therapists working in a parlor under a boss and be independent in establishing regulations.

Investing in a mobile massage therapy business eliminates expenses associated with a traditional office setup, such as the need for space-filling equipment and the salaries of a receptionist and manager; property insurance and electricity costs are also lowered with a mobile unit.

With the small private space provided by a mobile massage unit, therapists can offer couple massages, a sensual treat for many partners who can't enjoy the same togetherness at a parlor.

Also, a mobile unit enables entrepreneurs to visit homebound clients and those with disabilities. Even individuals with limited time can be seen in the privacy of the mobile massage unit, with the therapist setting an appointment near the client's business or residence.

There are, however, some disadvantages to having a mobile business as a massage therapist, such as having to pay higher self-employment taxes; being responsible for your health and vehicle insurance; incurring higher fuel and maintenance costs for the vehicle; commuting longer distances; and dealing with different client demands at odd hours, in addition to having to deal with advertising.

If you believe you got what it takes to succeed in the mobile massage therapy business, weigh the advantages and disadvantages and make a prudent decision. After all, nobody understands your needs better than you!

Ideas For Marketing Your Massage Therapy Business

All successful business tactics, such as sports massage therapy, mobile massage services or a professional massage studio, should incorporate a business-expanding marketing strategy. Your range of services, professional business methods and massage expertise can contribute to the development of a successful marketing strategy that is certain to attract new clients.

Online

Massage therapy provides different services, including shiatsu, sports therapy, Swedish and deep tissue massage. Provide your current and future consumers with a means to compare the alternatives and select your massage therapy facility or services as the superior option.

A web presence for your massage therapy business is the most effective method for acquiring new customers. You will be able to supply information and act as a resource for interested people, you will be discoverable through online directories and add user evaluations to boost your business's credibility and make the decision easier for your clients.

If you want to expand your internet presence further, continue to promote yourself as a resource by creating an interesting blog, RSS feed and an ongoing list of information for clients interested in massage therapy services.

Print

Print advertising tactics allow you to contact your targeted clients with special offers and branded advertisements that increase your customer base and brand recognition. Your print advertising should start with business cards that feature your logo and double as appointment reminders.

To expand your advertising chances, enlist the aid of your loyal clients by offering referral cards and a referral program that pays for their assistance. Postcards and flyers are a terrific way to contact people who might not otherwise be aware of your massage therapy business or be interested in it.

Postcards can be sent to your targeted clients using advertising lists that can be purchased, raising awareness of your business. Although customer return may not be 100 percent, it is a terrific method to create your brand and introduce customers to massage services.

Signs

Professional business procedures and specialist expertise define massage therapy. A professional and trustworthy appearance can be the determining element in a customer's firm selection.

If you operate out of a massage clinic or studio, your storefront creates the first image of your company. Establish a professional storefront with window signs that feature your logo and business tagline.

One-way vision is an excellent material that adds privacy to your clinic's windows and enables you to construct a

full-window advertisement that is full-color and visually striking. Your massage business windows should feature your
company's name, logo, and the studio's professionalism and
calming atmosphere.

Mobile marketing is the way to go if you provide mobile
massage services. When traveling between appointments,
car magnets are an ideal method of mobile advertising.
Simple, reusable advertising is a technique to boost the ef-
fectiveness of your other forms of advertising while promoting your services on the road.

Adding mobile advertising to your marketing plan can
yield unexpected benefits. Your consumer base will rise due
to the increased visibility of your brand and company name
in all formats.

Starting a massage therapy business is not a decision to
be taken lightly; it requires deliberation and the recognition
that it is a significant step in one's professional development.
For many, the decision provides financial independence, the
flexibility to work around family obligations and, often most
importantly, the fascinating challenges of running a business.

To make a suitable income from your massage therapist
salary, you will need a sufficient number of regular paying clients who consistently scheduled treatments. So, what methods should you employ to expand your client base?

Does advertising your massage business sound compli-
cated? Many of you can shudder at spending a fortune on
advertising and marketing and your lack of marketing expertise.

Let's get one thing straight: marketing your massage therapy business doesn't have to be complex or costly; it simply
entails promoting your company's name and services. How
can you expect people to arrange treatments if they are un-
aware of or have never heard of them?

Increasing your client base and, consequently, your massage therapist pay won't be simple; it will require a commit-

ment; therefore, don't expect your phone to start ringing with an influx of new customers if you do nothing.

Internet and creating a simple website or blog is an effective way to get started. If you go for a free web hosting platform, such as Blogger or Live Journal, it's quite simple and will cost you little or nothing.

Google AdWords is a relatively inexpensive method of advertising your massage business online, as it relies on potential customers clicking on ads presented in search engines and on other websites that are relevant to the things you will be giving.

Approaching organizations or groups, such as a mother and baby group, is typically an excellent, cost-free way to acquire customers. Instead of simply asking the organizers of the toddler group if you can leave business cards or fliers, you should attend a session in person, allowing you to present the treatment options, pricing, etc. to the mothers.

To optimize your massage therapist revenue, it doesn't seem like a good idea to perform treatments for free or at a discounted fee at the start of your career. This is not quite accurate; using this marketing strategy will often get people talking, not to mention spreading word of mouth. It is vital to target the appropriate persons for free treatments, such as those who work in large offices or organizations, shop owners and models.

These individuals interact daily with many possible customers, allowing them to mention your organization. After the treatment, be sure to distribute business cards to the customer so that they might pass them around.

CHAPTER 35

A PERSONAL STYLIST OR WARDROBE CONSULTANT

C elebrities, fashion models and actresses can't exist without fashion stylists. Since people are so occupied with their work today, many folks also choose to hire stylists. Most people today are fashion-conscious and strive to look their best at all times. This is one of the reasons why an increasing number of folks are utilizing the services of fashion and image consultants.

Fashion consultants collaborate closely with their customers to prepare them for events such as a catwalk, fashion shoots, film shoots or fashion shows. They effectively express their unique personalities through the selection of clothing and accessories.

Fashion stylists collaborate closely with prominent fashion designers, skilled hairstylists and makeup artists. Some stylists are also skilled in hair styling and produce stunning outcomes for their clients.

These stylists assist their clients in selecting the appropriate styles and colors while purchasing clothing and accessories. They fine-tune and stock their closets with attire that suits various circumstances. This is why they are often called personal shoppers.

People who fashion experts have styled stand out from the crowd and become the focal point of attention everywhere they go. Always poised and self-assured, they exude confidence and charisma. They are examples of high fashion that are expertly guided by their stylists, who assist them in keeping up with the always-evolving fashion trends.

Each successful stylist has their fashion website to facilitate client communication. Being a professional fashion stylist is a tough occupation that involves dedication and concentration. You can only become a reputable and successful stylist if you have a passion for designing and styling.

You can be a freelance, self-taught professional or pursue a degree from a reputable fashion college if you have the aptitude. Before striking out on your own, an apprenticeship with well-known fashion stylists greatly assists. This will help you learn the subtleties and tricks of the trade and gain an in-depth understanding of the industry.

You must be prepared to deal with demanding clients who insist on perfection. If you work with fashion models daily, you must be able to handle highly stressful scenarios that arise at the last minute.

A stylist employed by a television or film production unit must be skilled at selecting, planning and preparing objects that are ideally suited to each scene and circumstance. Before choosing the proper attire and accessories, one must remember the overall concept. Most of this must be accomplished with the budget in mind.

Also, fashion stylists must stay up with the most recent and current fashion trends. The key to your success is the skill with which you blend the personality and appearance of your clientele with the current fashion trends.

Expert fashion stylists can make last-minute repairs and quick modifications to garments with dropped hems or damaged seams. They will be able to pay close attention to the smallest details and have an extensive understanding of current fashion trends.

There are many stylists in this sector, so to withstand the competition and make a name for yourself as a reputable fashion stylist, you must possess persistence, concentration and, above all else, a strong passion for your work.

The salary of a personal stylist may vary significantly based on geographic region or project kind. As a business owner, you determine the price you charge and many stylists charge between $50 and $2,000 per hour, depending on their talents and the demand for their services.

Many personal stylists work part-time and may opt for a flat-rate pay structure. A stylist's daily prices might range from $500 to $750 for a half day to $1,000 to $1,500 for a full day. As the saying goes, the sky is the limit.

The first compensation for full-time entry-level stylists and interns may be less than $30,000 per year while they struggle to create a solid clientele. Mid-level stylists may expect to make a typical salary of $75,000 or more as they grow their portfolio, cultivate contacts and professional networks and improve their marketing and business savvy.

Suppose you continue to educate yourself and stay up-to-date with the market. In that case, you will build a solid client base with a trustworthy reputation and achieve professional status as a top-tier personal stylist. Consequently, you can earn more than $130,000 every year.

When answering the main question, "How much does a personal stylist make?" it is essential to note that a personal stylist's geographic location might considerably impact his or her salary. In larger cities, a stylist may charge $1,500 a day or earn between $65,000 and $125,000.

In contrast, less urban places may only be able to sustain a day rate of $500 to $750 or a salary of $30,000 to $45,000. New York and Los Angeles offer the highest salaries for stylists and image consultants, with Miami, London and Dubai also supporting a burgeoning sector.

The amount you can charge is also heavily dependent on your degree of talent and experience. Providing extra services, such as wardrobe styling and personal shopping, may also allow you to increase your rates.

The industry in which a stylist is employed is another consideration in deciding remuneration. You can offer personal styling and shopping services, become a retail fashion stylist, style for fashion shows and photo shoots or work in film and video styling.

Therefore, how much does a personal stylist earn? As you can see, as a freelance stylist, you define your value based on the time, travel and work you devote to each client.

CHAPTER 36

EVENT DJ OR ENTERTAINMENT SERVICES

Without any specific abilities, there are infinite ways to make incredibly good money entertaining youngsters. Every day, thousands of people in our country engage in this activity. Many engage in it full-time.

Also, many earn over $100,000 a year doing it. It is quite simple to entertain youngsters if you have a passion for them. There are countless opportunities to earn money while having a fantastic time. In addition, you should earn between $50 and $150 each hour.

In addition, no specific abilities, such as being a magician, clown or juggler, are required. I'm not talking about being an entertainer. I refer to bringing supplies, tools or equipment to an event and demonstrating how to have fun with them to children. What you provide to the children is what entertains them.

You can pursue a single or multiple concepts for your kids' entertainment business. There are dozens of different birthday party services for which you can give entertainment, for instance. Let me give you an example of a service that will generate revenue for you at festivals, business picnics, birthday parties and many other events.

When you combine this service with a few others, you will have a fantastic package of children's entertainment that will make you much easy money and anyone can accomplish it. Let me demonstrate only one concept.

SPIN ART - Children adore it! In Spin Art, children apply a few droplets of paint to a spinning card to create an original work of art. The card is placed within a frame for the child to take home and preserve.

There are two options available for spin art machines. One option is to spend between $225 and $395 for a commercial-grade, heavy-duty, motorized, ready-to-use spin art machine.

The cards slip pretty effortlessly into the holder; this is an excellent piece of equipment. These machines of commercial quality also permit the application of spin art to Frisbees. Later in this book, you will learn where to purchase the machines.

Another option is to purchase a battery-operated, non-commercial spin art machine from a toy store. There are many brands available on the market. You can find them in the catalogs you order or toy stores (Toys R Us, etc.)

You must purchase three at a cost between $16.00 and $20.00 apiece, utilizing two at a time and one as a backup. For larger crowds, utilize as many machines as necessary.

The commercial machine has a cardholder that the card easily slides into, whereas the non-commercial toy version has small tabs that the card corners must slide into. This hinders output.

In addition, you must clean each toy machine before storing it, being extremely careful not to get even a single drop of water into the spindle's hole. A single drop of water will corrode the small battery-powered motor, rendering the device useless.

The commercial versions are larger than the toy counterparts, which is an important factor during the first phase of your business.

Depending on whatever version you purchase, it is also slightly heavier and more bulky. Some are the size of a huge toy box or a trunk resembling a footlocker. Because the paint splatters against a cardboard insert or waste bag that lines the insert, no cleanup is required. It looks far more professional.

You should not worry about water entering the hole. It costs twenty times as much as the toy version. The cards enter and exit the cardholder much more quickly and the motor is more powerful, resulting in a significantly higher production rate.

The toy version is far less expensive, twenty times smaller and much lighter; however, it is more difficult to use due to the tabs that cards must be placed into and is difficult to clean after each use. They won't last anywhere near as long as the commercial version. They are produced at a slower rate than the commercial model.

They appear less professional but perform their duties adequately. This was my starting point. I recommend starting with the toy versions unless your budget and transport/storage issues are not an issue. Either option will suffice.

A youngster should only be permitted to squirt a few droplets of red, blue and yellow paint onto the card. Before the youngster squeezes the paint bottle, you must convey this information and ensure they adhere to it. If they apply too much paint on the card, it poses some issues.

Children should form a line before your two operating machines as they approach. Turn on the machine before the youngster squirts paint. After the youngsters have applied paint to the card, turn off the machine. Toy versions require considerable time to slow down. Don't wait for it. This slows down the entire procedure.

Place your finger on the spindle's outer edge to immediately slow it down. Remove the greeting card and place it in a frame. Staple the frame together. Insert another card into the tabs on the spindle and pass the dice to the next player.

Your startup spin art materials include cards, frames and paint. A firm offers the cards and frames in packs of 1,000 for approximately $125.00 at the time of writing. If you order above 5000, you will receive a discount.

The paint is often available for about $3.00 and $5.00 per quart at craft and school supply stores. You have approximately fifteen cents invested in each completed card and frame. Two dollars for this during a festival is an easy sale with a tremendous profit margin!

If too many options are available, the kids will take forever to decide which colors to use. (This also applies to snow cone syrup tastes if you are in the snow cone company.)

The only situation in which I would recommend expanding on this is if individual consumers are paying for the spin art. Stick to four colors for workplace picnics where everything is already paid for.

One quart of each will suffice for multiple gatherings. (Except for huge events.) Always bring extra paint and extra everything else as well. The paint is non-hazardous and water-based.

CHAPTER 37

BOUNCE KEYS HOUSE RENTAL

Suppose you are contemplating a business opportunity in the event rental and equipment area. In that case, you should be aware of a bounce house rental company that has become quite well-known and successful in this industry.

The main advantage of renting inflatables for occasions is that youngsters will enjoy themselves for hours with less effort. The challenge of preparing a birthday party for children is much reduced for a parent who doesn't need to come up with an extensive list of games to keep the children entertained. Parents like being able to relax while their children enjoy themselves.

As this entertainment is often used at community and corporate events, the rental industry has experienced phenomenal expansion. It is simple to start your own business because all you need is one high-quality inflatable. Many businesses of this nature start with a single system and grow as they gain experience and reputation in their areas.

Creating a plan is one of the most essential phases in growing a business. Create an appealing business name that conveys your mission. Determine appropriate rates in light of regional tendencies. Look for advertising possibilities that will allow you to maintain minimal expenditures while acquiring community recognition.

Consider that your equipment extends beyond the inflatable while you do research. You should consider your equipment transportation needs, keeping a hand truck and trailer on hand for efficient transfer of your inflatable. Also required are the proper installation tools, such as extension cords, sandbags, anchors and hammers.

It is exciting to purchase a single entertainment system and launch a business. You can get the necessary experience locating clients and meeting their demands by starting on a modest scale. This is an opportunity to gain knowledge of the sector without being overwhelmed. You will acquire accustomed to the time required for equipment setup and removal.

Also, you will acquire acquainted with customer interests. As you listen to their questions, you can receive insight into potential equipment additions. In the beginning, limiting the scope of your inventory is advantageous. A simple bounce house is ideal for the new company.

Before diversifying, you can wish to improve your supply of essentials as your business grows. You can add themed houses or combined bounce house designs later. There are many entertaining options available on the market nowadays and it is essential to leverage consumer enthusiasm as a guide for expansion.

One of the most significant aspects of expanding your business is obtaining high-quality bounce houses for sale. Some prospective company founders believe that department store bouncers will put them on the fast track to success.

Still, the reality is that commercial equipment and home entertainment options are vastly different. Different prices exist for a purpose and a reputable company will offer durable inflatables.

There are many avenues to pursue in the bounce house industry. Others provide on-site supervision but some organizations just install equipment and leave their systems in place for predetermined lengths of time.

Others build an entertainment experience firm, while some simply rent their equipment. Others build pay-to-play businesses, setting up at community carnivals, fairs and festivals. The business is intriguing because there are many opportunities.

Party planning should be at the top of the list for folks keen to launch a full-time or part-time business. If you are outgoing, energetic and want to have fun while working hard, you can want to investigate the potential for starting a bounce house rental business. Click the link above to talk with an expert.

CHAPTER 38

VOICEOVER OR ACTING

If you are contemplating starting a voice-over business, you must evaluate the obstacles you will face and the potential rewards. Here are few suggestions for launching a voice-over business.

Do what you enjoy.

This is often the first thought that comes to mind when individuals consider starting a business: the possibility of making a living doing something I truly enjoy and am passionate about. I'm assuming that, as a voiceover artist, you have this enthusiasm since if you don't love what you do, it will be extremely difficult to create a successful career with it.

This applies to anyone pursuing a creative business, including voiceover, acting, film directing, musicianship and writing. The creative industries are tremendously competitive and difficult to break into; without a passion for your work and confidence in your abilities, you will struggle to generate any money, much alone enough to support yourself and your family.

Also, remember that you will be investing so much time and effort in starting and growing your voiceover career that it is essential that you enjoy what you do now and remember this when you encounter difficult circumstances.

Now that we know you're passionate get rid of it. Step back and think objectively. Can you transform your voice-over hobby into a lucrative business? Exists a need for your voice? Through your passion as a voiceover artist, you have likely already conducted this market research without realizing it.

Even for the most distinctive and strange voices, projects and companies are looking for your sound if you look hard enough. Consider whether these initiatives will be frequent and profitable enough to provide a living. If not, what options do you have? Change jobs? Alternatively, you could seek training to strengthen your range and expertise to increase your employment as a voice actor.

The business plan

Writing a business strategy for your voiceover profession can be highly beneficial. I must admit that I did not do this immediately. Still, it is a useful exercise for focusing the mind, adopting a professional mindset and defining what you want to accomplish, how and when. It is also a wonderful chance to daydream! They are beneficial to have as your business evolves and develops.

Different general business templates are available on the Internet, and a voiceover artist-specific template is available at voices.com. A business plan is also essential to raise capital via a bank loan or overdraft. Investors want to see their investments in black and white. In addition, finance takes me to my next point.

Finances

How much money will you require, for what purpose and how will you acquire it? With the credit crunch appearing unwilling to abate, obtaining external financing through bank loans and investors is more tough than it used to be. Therefore, you must analyze your possibilities. First, why do you require the funds? You will need money to pay your bills and eat until your firm becomes profitable.

According to some, a business takes roughly three years to become truly established and earn a respectable income. Therefore, having funds, a second job or, like many others, a very understanding partner or spouse with a stable salary!

What else do you require financing for? A home studio is a must for most voice actors. There have been many articles, blogs and podcasts about home studio equipment and their prices, which I won't repeat here.

You don't need all the fancy equipment when you're just starting. Start small and expand your equipment chain as your knowledge and expertise increase. My first voiceover assignments were performed without a suitable microphone!

I captured the audio with a Sony digital video camera and editing software! The audio quality wasn't great but earned me employment and helped me expand my portfolio and bank account so I could afford better equipment! Consider Harlan Hogan's $129 portable studio booth.

What more could you want? He even has an article with directions on how to build one yourself; see harlanhogan. com for more information. Consider carefully and spend prudently - do you truly need ISDN services immediately? So let's examine other startup expenses.

Establishment expenses, including company cards, website design, domain registration, hosting, office equipment, advertising and marketing expenses and many more

Determine what you need now, what you would like to have in the future and what you can go without.

Also, consider your abilities and what you can do to save money - do you need a website designer? Can you construct a simple site using FrontPage or why not get an inexpensive web template that you can customize? Is there any goods or services for which you can trade your voiceover services?

Why not inquire with your local printers about the possibility of receiving free business cards or letterheads in exchange for recording their phone greetings or website audio? And always compare prices on the Internet for whatever you require; Vistaprint offers a fantastic selection of free business cards and inexpensive promotional postcards.

Professional conduct Be professional right away.

Everything about you and your business practices must communicate that you are a serious professional.

Obtain business cards, a work phone number with voice-mail and an appropriate business email address and obtain expert assistance - it doesn't take long to realize that running a voiceover business isn't just about being a voiceover actor - you are now responsible for a vast array of tasks, including bookkeeping, sales & marketing and administration. Some of these chores would greatly benefit from expert assistance; if you're not an accountant, get one; if you need to draft a contract, employ an attorney.

This also applies to tax and legal matters: it's much simpler (and cheaper) to get these things in order from the start rather than to clean up a mess afterward. Whether setting up as a sole proprietor or forming a business will affect your tax liability and the amount of VAT you can pay. It is advisable to seek professional assistance from your local tax office to obtain all the necessary information and forms.

Consider joining organizations and unions for professionals. Also worth investigating is your local small business organization, where you can stay abreast of the most recent general business practices and where networking opportunities abound.

CHAPTER 39

PASTA MAKING

To establish a business creating homemade pasta, you must first understand the fundamentals of making fresh pasta. This pasta uses fresh ingredients and has a shorter shelf life than commercially produced or dried pasta.

Producing fresh pasta is preferable because the manufacturer can personalize the pasta to the individual consumer's shape, size, color and flavor preferences

The steps for launching a homemade pasta manufacturing firm are: First Stage, Regulatory Compliance and Marketing.

First Process

- Develop and improve a recipe that you believe will sell and yield identical results each time it is prepared. Taste them with your family and friends and solicit their opinions.

- As with any business, when establishing a business creating homemade pasta, you should create a business plan including your objectives and financial projections. This will guide you in the real operation of the firm and help you determine if it is successful.

Purchase your ingredients and materials, such as bags and packaging materials. Determine how you'll package your homemade pasta. It might be packaged in a freezer-safe bag so that consumers can freeze, refrigerate or enjoy the product immediately. It may also be packaged in cellophane bags. You could search online for wholesale distributors of these products.

You can save money and create a professional and uniform appearance. You can design and print your labels using a computer or have a professional designer produce them for you and purchase them in quantity. Include cooking and serving directions on food product labels.

- Acquire equipment you don't currently possess to produce huge quantities of your recipes much quicker and simpler.

- Compile a list of wholesale prices for all your products. Consider all costs associated with producing homemade pasta, including ingredients, facilities, packaging and labor.

This should be presented in the form of a spreadsheet that includes both the retail and wholesale prices for each of your products.

Regulatory Conformity

- Since you will be starting a homemade pasta manufacturing business and creating a food product, you must contact your local and state health offices to inquire about the necessary permits and licenses.

- Ensure that you can legally sell the products you make in your home kitchen, as different states have varying regulations governing homemade food products. You can access this information online through your state's Department of Health website or request a hard copy. Check local zoning restrictions to see if conducting a home-based business is permitted.

\Alabama, Iowa, Indiana, Kentucky, Maine, New Hampshire, North Carolina, Ohio, Pennsylvania, Tennessee, Vermont, Virginia and Utah are the only states that permit the establishment of home-based cooking businesses as of 2010. Therefore, you must investigate these before launching a firm.

- Most states permit selling homemade food items at farmers' and flea markets without the required state licenses and inspections.

They only permit the sale of these items at these locations. Make sure your state doesn't have any label requirements, such as "Made in a home kitchen and not inspected by the (insert state's) Department of Agriculture," before starting a homemade pasta-making business and selling your products in these locations.

Check your state's cottage laws regarding the labeling requirements for homemade products. The label should include the product's name and the ingredients utilized.

- Most home-based food preparation businesses are either sole proprietorships or partnerships. If you intend to make your business your primary source of income, a DBA (Doing Business As) license is your best option if you will name your company.

Marketing

- Your primary rival in the homemade pasta industry is commercial pasta. Consequently, competing supermarkets and grocery stores is not a smart idea, as is not a smart idea To attract clients, you must employ tried-and-true marketing techniques, such as distributing posters and leaflets.

Make your business known in your neighborhood by distributing complimentary pasta dish samples made with your fresh pasta at community gatherings and meetings.

During these events, it is also beneficial to customize your fresh pasta to meet the specific needs of each consumer. If you enjoy preparing healthy pasta, you can attempt to sell your creations at local health food stores.

Local farmer's markets, artisan festivals and flea markets are viable alternatives for selling your goods. Many enjoy the flavor of homemade goods, such as fresh pasta but lack time to cook them themselves.

You can provide them with the homemade flavor they desire. During holidays and special events, many individuals enjoy giving local and homemade foods as presents.

- You can also market your food products by making your brochures, catalogs and price lists and by selling them in retail stores that sell local goods. Compile a list of your community's target retailers with the contact information of the person in charge of purchasing.

- Ask local Italian restaurants if they purchase pre-made pasta, as this could be an opportunity for a joint venture between your firm and theirs.

- The Internet is also an excellent medium for promoting your products nationally. If possible, you might create your website to aid in the expansion of your firm.

These procedures should assist you in launching a home-made pasta business.

CHAPTER 40.

LOCAL DELIVERY OR COURIER SERVICES

Almost all businesses utilize parcel delivery services at some time. Theoretically, it is a simple business to start if you only collect and distribute packages locally. However, if you are serious about establishing a competitive parcel delivery firm, you must consider it.

First, while you can acquire a few local businesses as customers, the likelihood is that all of them will at some point require national or international parcel delivery. You can't meet this standard alone if you are just starting in the parcel delivery industry.

Consequently, you will 3need to subcontract a portion of the task, which will necessitate establishing agreements with national carriers.

You will also need to make preparations for insurance, as you won't only need to insure your parcel delivery van but, more significantly, its contents.

While it will be simple to obtain blanket insurance coverage, you must ensure that the value of your customers' packages doesn't exceed the limits of your policy or inform your clients that their items are only protected up to a certain amount.

When establishing a parcel courier business, you will also need to consider fuel costs, van depreciation and van operating expenses.

In addition, you will need to set up client billing and consider how you will handle deliveries if you become unwell or your van breaks down.

While establishing a parcel delivery service may appear simple, other factors must be considered.

Establishing a van delivery or courier delivery service from home is one of the most effective ways for an entrepreneur to enter the business sector. Better than that, in many ways, is that it can be accomplished without needing third-party assistance. In business, independence is a great asset.

First, there is a low cost; the demand for van delivery services is anticipated to remain indefinitely. Busy mothers, anxious professionals and time-crunched students often seek assistance delivering items to their homes and offices.

There are few things you'll need before starting. A van should be a given but it is also essential to have a computer, a printer and a cell phone. For many individuals, contacting a landline is also essential; it lends credibility and permanence to proceedings, especially for the elderly. When delivering for your consumers, trust is an absolute must.

While any roadworthy van would suffice, you will make a considerably better first impression (and perform better) if you can get your hands on something attractive. Depending on your budget, it may be worthwhile to place essential information (such as your name and phone number) on the side of the van for advertising purposes.

After organizing this, you must focus on more advertising. People need to be aware of you and your van delivery business; create a flier on your home computer. Using ordinary software and free photographs, it should not take too long and pretty professional magazines can be created for free.

Then, you must determine where to distribute these flyers; colleges, retirement/nursing homes and retail parks are all acceptable starting areas. Also consider your local retailers.

Attempt to create a timetable that maximizes your revenue when you receive your first reservations; invest in mapping software and plan your route to many destinations. You will also be better positioned to accept (more lucrative) last-minute employment.

CONCLUSION

Starting a side business can be an exciting way to make more income and explore your interests but it can also require a substantial time and energy commitment. There are some choices to explore if you want to launch a side business with minimal time and effort.

One possibility is to launch a dropshipping business in which things are sold online without needing to physically handle inventories. You can choose a specialized product and collaborate with a supplier to list their products on your website through dropshipping. The supplier handles shipping and fulfillment when an order is placed, leaving you to focus on marketing and selling the products.

Another possibility for a low-effort side company is to offer freelancing services in a specialized field. This may include visual design, social media management and writing and editing. You can pick when and how much you work as a freelancer, making it a flexible and low-effort option.

Consider delivering workshops or lessons as a side business if you are passionate about a certain activity or interest. If you enjoy cooking, you might provide cooking classes or meal prep packages for busy people. This allows you to share your talents and passions with others while simultaneously earning money.

Start a blog or YouTube channel focusing on a specific topic or specialty as a low-effort business. You can monetize your material through advertising, sponsorships and other means.

Regardless of the side company idea you choose, it is essential to conduct research and plan thoroughly. This will ensure that your side business is successful and doesn't consume excessive time and effort. You can develop a successful side business that allows you to pursue your passions and produce other cash without burning yourself with a little strategy and determination.